GREATNESS OF GOD

Luthando Ningiza

<u>Other Works by Author:</u>

God of Mankind

TABLE OF CONTENTS

DEDICATION

I would like to dedicate this book to all those who have lost hope, saying deep down in their hearts *"there is no God "*, because of the things they have encountered in this world.

ACKNOWLEDGEMENT

My special thanks, appreciation and acknowledgement goes to the following people:

* I would like to thank my Lord my God in Jesus Christ name, who gave me the mind and the idea of a vision to start writing, He kept pouring in me what I should say and write it down. I didn't know what to do or say, but He stood there by my side and helped me to come to the end of this book. Thank You God!

* I would like also to give my great gratitude to the most five important people in my life: My children, my son **Reyaoboka {Reya} Rankutu** and my daughter **Mandilive { live } Mavume** . To my mother, **Lydia Dokazi Ningiza**, my brother **Anele Ningiza**, and my sister **Yonela Ningiza** .They managed to give me enough time and space to sit down and write this book without disturbing me until the day I finished it.

May God my Lord be with them at all times.

* People who were so close to me, in thick and hard times of my life, from the day I was born. I can't stop remembering you in my prayers, Pambo family at Ezibeleni Township (Queenstown). **Mr Robert Mxolisi Pambo**, **Mrs Maureen Nokhaya Pambo** (aunt), the late **Zukiswa Pambo**(RIP); **Lizo Pambo,Nelisa Pambo** and **Mfundo Pambo**.

* My aunt **Nombulelo Gladys Ningiza** and your children.

* Thanks to my local Church leadership and Pastor, **Mr. Mjongisi Mpotololo** for your prayers, guidance and support.

* I didn't know you, you didn't know me, yet you welcomed and open your arms for me to be the shoulder to cry on. You were there for me. I thank you brothers. God be with you always. **Mr. Mpumelelo Danny Mbanyana** and his family.

* **Mr. James Makeleni** and his family.

* Special sincere thanks also goes to **Mr. Tsepo Rankutu**, for all your efforts and time in assisting me. God bless you.

* People who help me in managing to publish this book.

* Audience at large. I Thank you all.

INTRODUCTION

About the Book

If it was not because of God's Love and His righteousness towards man, the world would have been long time destroyed by God, but his righteousness stopped and held him from destroying the world.

Instead of doing so, he wanted what He belongs to him back and to build a strong relationship love affair with man once and for all. What separated man from God was the sin that man did, and where there is sin God packs and goes and the sin leads a man to destruction that will lead him to eternal condemnation.

The only thing that will help man to have a strong bond with God is through crucifying the flesh, put away the misdeeds of the flesh and leave by the spirit, living by the spirit it will help to grow in the Lord.

When you have grown in the Lord, it is then that you will know what to do and not to do to please Him, growing in the Lord will help in building the character of a person that God want out of you.

The character that is built in you will help you to discover yourself to be a better person that God wants and is expecting out of you as a Christian, that you were not just saved for absolutely no good reason.

But you were saved for a purpose; to serve God's people. When serving God's people, you take lead, you make initiatives; when taking initiatives, you expect good reward out of all that you have been toiling for, because you know that your labour in the Lord is not in vain. {1Corinthians15:58}

The Aims of the Book

The aim of this book is to reveal God's heart at his best towards man on earth. His endless love towards man and what is in store for man in God's heart, and also aiming in building a strong and unshakeable relationship towards man and God the creator.

It is aiming at reviving and challenging man and woman of God to come back to their senses, and to serve God in a manner that is worth pleasing and acceptable to God.

It is also challenging man and woman of God, to have a deep introspection into their daily lives and search themselves if they still live according to the standard of what they claim to be or they are just doing a Lip service.

The book also aims at motivating, inspiring and encouraging man and woman of God, young and old that surely there is a future hope for them. Stop doubting God and believe.

To whom who was and He is and will always be; may the grace of our Lord Jesus Christ, the love of God and the fellowship of the Holy Spirit, be with you all. Amen.

REFERENCES:

All Bible verses were quoted from:
NIV BIBLE AND **HOLY BIBLE.** {King James Version}

GREATNESS OF GOD

God's Righteousness

From the beginning of the earth, God was there. Nothing on earth came out of itself, and nothing came without God allowing it. The life we live today started with God and it will end with Him. He is the Alpha and Omega. The beginning and the end of everything, so as we the human, we were made by Him, God is the maker of man.

" .... Let us make man in our own image and in our own likeness and let him rule over the earth...". {Genesis 1:26 - 27}

Here we saw how the first man came on earth, his original background. A man was made by God in His own image on earth.

Why there was a need and necessity for God to create a man in his own image? After God has created all the things on earth: plants, animals and all that is in it.

So God saw that it was good for Him to create something now that would look similar to Him as God. And as God the creator, since He is up above in heaven His throne. It was on

His wish to have something similar to Him, that can be His steward here on earth, to come and rule the earth.

Also, the very same plants and animals He had created, He did not want them to praise and worship him, so God felt that there must be something that will bow and worship him on earth while He is up there in heaven His throne. And the very same thing that He wanted it to bow on Him. He felt that!

That thing that will bow and worship him. It must be something that will resemble Him and have similarities as Him {God}.

It must have certain special powers to all the things He as God created on earth, so there can be a reason for it to worship Him and also him as God since He created, but did not want to rule the earth.

He decided to make something similar to Him that contains His likeness. So He formed up the man through His image. It is no wonder we see God asking Jeremiah to call on Him, and man is the only creation that the Lord God spoke with, out of all the created things that God created.

" Call to me and I will answer you and tell you great and unsearchable things you do not know" {Jeremiah 33:3}

"They exchanged the truth of God for a lie and worshiped and served created things rather than the Creator who is forever praised. Amen" {Romans 1:25}

That is why we say a man was formed in order to worship and praise Him. So God formed up the man and breathed through his nostrils.

"Then God said, ' Let us make man in Our image, according to Our likeness; let them have dominion over the fish of the sea, over birds of the air and over the cattle, over all the earth and over creeping thing that creeps on earth " {Genesis 1: 26 }

"And the Lord God formed man of the dust of the ground, and breathed into his nostrils the breath of life; and a man became a living being" {Genesis2:7}

So the part of making was of God, but the part of ruling was of man. But the man failed to practice and to put it into reality the role he was created to do. The man's failure to practice his powers led him to be deceived by what he was supposed to be in control of it. The man's failure to practice his powers of dominion led him to sin that separated him and God.

A man realised that they have done something that was out

of the will of their creator. The man tried to hide from God because man saw himself naked to be seen by God. The Lord asked them why they are hiding themselves, and their reason was that they were naked so their nakedness made them to be ashamed of themselves more than what they have failed to do.

When God my Lord heard their excuse, He asked them who told them that they were naked, because to Him as God, of all the things he said to them, He never told or said to them that they were naked, so where did they get that now?

"And he said, 'Who told you that you were naked? Have you eaten from the tree which I commanded you not to eat?'" {Genesis3:11}.

Then Adam explain to God what happened. So God went to the woman to confront her of what she has done.

"And the Lord God said to the woman, 'What is this you have done?'. The woman said, "The serpent deceived me, and I ate". {Genesis 3: 13}

That question alone that God asked the woman 'What *is this you have done?'*, that shows and reveals the heart of God. The feeling He was encountering concerning what happened.

That question was an emotional painful question that God was feeling about what happened. So God gave to each one of them from the serpent the snake, to Adam and Eve their punishment for what they have done.

After He punished them God showed his first righteousness towards man, His love by dressing them to cover their nakedness. For He is a good caring loving God.

"The Lord God made garments of skin for Adam and his wife and clothed them." {Genesis3:21}

In the scriptures, the Bible {Book of Job}, there is a very interesting question whereby we see Job having a concerned question to God about a man; after the experiences him as Job, he had undergone through in his life:

"What is man that you make so much of him, that you give him so much attention" {Job 7:17}.

When God breathed His breath to a man, God was entering into earth in a form of a man; That means in a man, there is God in him, because he gave life to man.

So that is a reason why God is giving a man so much attention and care, because of the fact that, in a man there is

Him. So if God lives in us through His Spirit, His Spirit testifies with our Spirit that we are God's children.

"The Spirit himself testify with our spirit that we are Gods children " *{Romans 8:16}*

That shows we have the same spirit in us as God. If we share the same Spirit with God, that will mean that His Spirit intercedes with our Spirit.

"And He who searches our hearts knows the mind of the Spirit, because the Spirit intercedes for the saints in accordance with Gods will". *{Romans 8:27}*

Also, God called a man by his name:

" Fear not, for I have redeemed you; I have summoned you by name". *{Isaiah43:1}*

Because in a man there is Him, that is a reason why He even said to Jeremiah that:

"He does not have the plans to harm man but to prosper him" *{Jeremiah 29:11}*

Why...?

For HE is not a parent who can give birth to a child with the aim to destroy and to see the child suffering. And also, God shows that He have plans for us; He did not just create us for no good reason, but to fulfil His plans. Also, God provided a man with something to eat and something to do on the land he provided to him.

To all that God he did for a man after He created him. God put a man in a garden called Eden. As God put a man in a garden of Eden, He told a man that he can eat everything except one thing, that one thing; that was a tree that was in the centre of the garden of Eden.

A man was told by God of what the consequences of eating will be. But man failed to hold on to God's command through serpent deception and ate to the tree of knowledge of good and evil.

"When the woman saw that the fruit of the tree was good for food, and pleasing to the eye, and also desirable for gaining wisdom, she took some and ate it. She also gave some to her husband, who was with her, and he ate it." {Genesis3:6}

So that was the fall of a man away from God and the sin

entered on earth; the sin that separated man from God. As that tree was a tree of knowledge of good and evil. So God saw that now a man knows what He knows, Him as God, and He decided to banished them away from the garden of Eden.

The reason was to prevent a man from also eating to the tree of life that can make them live for ever.

"And the Lord God said " The man has now became like one of us, knowing good and evil. He must not be allowed to reach out his hand and take also from the tree of life and eat, and live forever" {Genesis 3:22}

After the man Adam ate to that tree, there were consequences that led them to be banished from Eden and then death was introduced by not allowing man to have an access to the tree of life. That meant a man won't live for ever, he will die. A man called Adam disobeyed what the Lord has said to him, and the punishment was death.

It's not only the man Adam, but every human being was affected. So God punished man with death so that he cannot live forever:

" So for one man's offence, death reigns on earth and the laws were put into place over a man through Moses" "For if, by the trespass of the one man, death reigned through that one

man, how much more will those who receive God's abundant provision of grace and of the gift of righteousness reign in life through the one man, Jesus Christ ". {Romans 5:17:}

If you look in the old testament there are many laws that are there that were introduced. Those laws were introduced to control and restricting people in living and how to please God. Some of the familiar laws are the *Ten Commandments;* that we all know.

Those laws were put in order to control man, and the people went into covenants with God, but those laws and covenants never prevented and saved man from death and being separated from God. So the people of God continued to be separated from God and dying.

In all that, God never stopped walking with man either. Instead God was always with his people, in spite of the wrong doing they have done. He kept on protecting His people. Yet we were the ones who kept drifting away from God because of our iniquities.

" But the Lord said to him, "Not so; if anyone kills Cain, he will suffer vengeance seven times over", Then the Lord put a mark on Cain so that no one who found him would kill him. So Cain went out from the Lord's presence and lived in the land of

Nod, east of Eden". {Genesis 4:15-16}

In God seeing what He has made with his own hands in his own image drifting and perishing, He was not happy at all, He was hurt. Like any parent who sees his children not listening but perishing, so as GOD himself, he felt the pain of losing his children. And He cried.

Some will argue why I say God "He Cried"; if you can notice, and you can look carefully to the verse below, the sound of it clearly shows and reveals to us the painful situation that God was experiencing deep down.

"I reared children and brought them up, but they have rebelled against me" {Isaiah 1:2}

Should a parent talk like this, that means he/she is crying deep down. No wonder you see me say God was crying. This is the second time where we see God, how He feels about man.

But because of the love He has for His people, He called up to them to come up and reason with him, because the sin has separated man from God. Since a man is a creation of God in His likeness and in man there is Spirit of God so God cannot decide about man because a man himself knows the good and the wrong.

So God wanted to bring back what belongs to Him and called to His people so there can be peace and mutual understanding between Him and man.

"Come now, let us reason together; said the Lord " {Isaiah 1:18}.

"If my people, who are called by my name, will humble themselves and pray and seek my face and turn from their wicked ways, I will hear from heaven and will forgive their sin I will heal their land " {2 Chronicles 7:14}

God's love for man could not make Him to relax and keep quiet in seeing his creation perishing and decided that He will send a saviour who will redeem His people from the wrath; and God, because of his love for us, He started to reveal what is He going to do.

"Surely the sovereign Lord does nothing without revealing his plan to his servants the prophets" {Amos3:7}.

He showed all his plans about man and revealed it through Micah and to the prophet Isaiah; who he was; and how and where this saviour will come from and Isaiah prophesied about him, and let it known to people.

"Therefore the Lord himself will give you a sign: The virgin will be with child and will give a birth to a son, and will call him Immanuel " {Isaiah 7:14}

and

"For to us a child is born, to us a son is given, and the government will be on his shoulders. And He will be called wonderful counsellor, Mighty God, Everlasting Father, Prince of Peace". {Isaiah 9:6}

"But you, Bethlehem Ephrathah, though you are small among the clans of Judah, out of you will come for me one who will be ruler over Israel, whose origins are from of old, from ancient times" {Micah 5:2}

Also, God revealed of how and where this Redeemer will come from:

"A shoot will come up from the stump of Jesse; from his roots a Branch will bear fruit. The Spirit of the Lord will rest on him--the Spirit of wisdom and of understanding, the Spirit counsel and of power, the Spirit of knowledge and of the fear of

the Lord----and he will delight in the fear of the Lord. He will not judge by what he sees with his eyes, or decide by what he hears with his ears; but with righteousness he will judge the needy, with justice his will give decisions for the poor of the earth. He will strike the earth, with the rod of his mouth; with the breath of his lips he will slay the wicked. Righteousness will be his belt and faithfulness the sash around his waist. 10) "In that day the Root of Jesse will stand as a banner for the peoples; the nations will rally to him, and his place of rest will be glorious. In that day the Lord will reach out his hand a second time to reclaim the remnant that is left of his people from Assyria, from Lower Egypt, from Upper Egypt, from Cush, from Elam, from Babylonia, from Hamath and from the islands of the sea". {Isaiah 11:1-5. & 10-11}

Why from the shoot of Jesse?

Since the serpent used woman to bring sin on earth, so God saw a need for Him also to use a woman to bring the saviour on earth and not a man, Why not a man? Since the sin came on earth through the weakness of a woman so shall the saver came through the Spiritual strong point of a woman.

"And Adam was not the one deceived and became a sinner. It was a woman who was deceived and became a sinner. But

woman will be saved through child bearing if they continue in faith, love and holiness with propriety" {1 Timothy 2:14-15.}

If you look back from the creation, God gave man the powers and the dominion over all things on earth and rule and govern. So God has shuttered himself on the affairs of the earth because He has entrusted man with dominion, but man failed to practice his powers because he fell into a trap that deceived Eve.

" and let them rule over the fish of the sea, and the birds of the air, over livestock, over all the earth and over all the creatures that move along the ground" {Genesis 1:26}.

In order for God to interfere again in the affairs of this world, He had to have à plan, the only plan to be involve on earth affairs was to come himself in a form of a man, born from the man. So God showed to the prophets how He would come and what signs will we know that He has come:

" A voice of one calling: "In the desert prepare the way for the Lord; make straight in the wilderness a high way for our God ". {Isaiah 40:3}.

Because of the Lord's great love, we are not consumed, for his compassion never fails. And as we have seen what He did for Cain in Genesis 4; that is the kind of God we are serving. That is why we say with confidence that His mercy are new every morning; great is His faithfulness and when God speaks everything he says; happens, he said he will punish man and really a man was punished, now God wants to save his people from the sin and no one can change that.

"Because of the Lords great love we are not consumed; for his compassion never fail. They are new every morning". {Lamentations 3:22-23}

"Who can speak and have it happen if the Lord has not decreed it? It is not from the mouth of the Most High that both calamities and good things to come." {Lamentations 3:37-38}

When God saw his people falling away, he felt that He could not relax, sit down and fold his arms and give the devil an upper arm over to His people.

"For the mountains shall depart and the hills be removed, but My Kindness shall not depart from you, Nor shall my covenant of peace be removed, Says the Lord, who has mercy on you." {Isaiah 54:10}

"I myself will search for my sheep and look after them. As a Shepherd looks after his scattered flocks when he is with them, so will I look after my sheep. I will rescue them from all the places where they were scattered on a day of clouds and darkness" {Ezekiel 34:11-12}

All this happened because of His great righteousness, and the love He has for His people. Truly we are serving an awesome merciful, righteous God Almighty, Who by His love and mercy opened up a fountain.

We all know that a fountain is where we found water; water can be used for washing dirty and for drinking. So the people were thirsty and burning deep down in their lives by their sins they were also dirty in the eyes of the Lord.

"In that day a fountain shall be opened for the house of David and for the inhabitants of Jerusalem, for sin and for uncleanness" {Zechariah 13:1-2}

His love endures forever!

For God so loved the world. He gave up his son so that all those who believed in him may not perish but have an everlasting life.

Why God so loved the world? Because, in the world there was some precious cargo which was carrying him as God himself. So he couldn't watch and see that which contains him perishing while he is watching. Our bodies are that precious cargo, it is no wonder the word tells us that our bodies is the temple of the Holy Spirit that live inside us.

"Do you not know that your body is the temple of the Holy Spirit , who is in you, whom you have received from God ? You are not your own." {1 Corinthians 6: 19}

That was a reason why He gave up His son.

"For God so loved the world that he gave his only Son that whoever believes in him shall not perish but have eternal life" *{John 3:16 }*

"And God was reconciling the world to himself in Christ, not counting men's sins against them. And he has committed to us the message of reconciliation." *{ 2 Corinthians 5:19 }*

Gods image is not merely a form; God's image is:

- o *Love,*
- o *Righteousness,*
- o *Holiness,*

- o *Purity,*
- o *Gentleness,*
- o *Kindness and*
- o *Goodness.*

I know some will wonder why I use some of the fruits of the Spirit as they are mentioned in the book of Galatians as the Gods image. If we care to know, first of all, we will understand that God is Spirit, and if God is the spirit, surely you have to find all of the above.

"God is Spirit, and his worshipers must worship in spirit and in truth." {John 4: 24}

All of the above they make God completely to be what he is {Spirit}. The bible tells us to worship God in Spirit and in truth. So that very same Spirit that he want us to worship him with, is the same Spirit He breathed on us. That makes us to be the image of what He wanted us to be.

"So God created man in His own image, in the image of God there is man. He created Him male and female." {Genesis1:26-27}

Jesus Christ the lamb came in a form of a man, but still in

Him. He retained the very same image likeness of God.

When he came, there were laws that were in place, those laws were from God through Moses and other prophets. So when Jesus Christ came; He came with a new and the last law, so what does that mean? Does it mean that the first laws that came through Moses and the prophets no longer have effect?

In the beginning. God said:

"Let us make man in our own image"

Whose image is that?

Well that is: *"Trinity "*

"God the father, God the Son and God the Holy Spirit".

So a man was created through this image, that shows us that God the Son, was there before the creation; He was God and He was with God; Jesus himself is the image of the living God, that means He is the Alpha and Omega. And Paul the Apostle also emphasises that:

"He is the image of the invisible God, and first-born over-all creation. For by him all things were created: things in heaven and on earth, visible and invisible, whether thrones or powers or rulers or authorities; all things were created by him and for him. He is before all things, and in him all things hold together

" *and "For God was pleased to have all his fullness dwell in him"* {Colossians 1:15-17 and 19}

The proof of what we hear from Paul, we see it from Jesus Himself when He says to his disciples:

"Jesus answered, ' Don't you know me, Philip, even after I have been among you such a long time? Anyone who has seen me has seen the Father. How can you say, ' Show us the Father'?" {John 14:9}

"In the beginning was the word, and the word was with God, and the Word was God. He was with God in the beginning. Through him all things were made; without him nothing was made that has been made. In him was life, and that life was the light of men. The light shines in the darkness, but the darkness has not understood it" 14: *"The word became flesh and made his dwelling among us. We have seen his glory, the glory of the One and Only who came from the Father, full of grace and truth* " {John 1:1-5 & 14}

His coming, it was not revealed to Isaiah only but also to a man of Jerusalem by the name of Simeon, He was told that he won't see or experience death before he sees the Lord Christ and really the man did see the Lord Christ when He was presented at the temple.

Also, an 84 years old prophetic widow by the name of Anna, who was serving God with prayers and fasting in the temple witnessed the Christ the Lord:

26: "And it had been revealed to him by the Holy Spirit that He would not see death before he had seen the Lord Christ" & 38: *"coming up to them at that very moment, she gave thanks to God and spoke about the child {Jesus Christ} to all who were looking forward to the redemption of Jerusalem" {Luke 2:26 &38}*

He also was seen by John the Baptist while he was still baptizing. He revealed him to the people.

"The next day John saw Jesus coming toward him, and he said, "Behold! The Lamb of God who takes away the sin of the world!" {John 1:29 }

As Jesus went to be baptised also by John, and to John it felt so strange that how come he as a creation, baptise his creator and Jesus Christ told him to do so in order to fulfil all righteousness.

Do you still remember that, In order for God to interfere

again in the affairs of this world, He had to have à plan, the only plan to be involve on earth affairs was to come himself in a form of a man, born from the man? So that was a reason why Jesus have to be baptised also. At that particular moment the heavens declared and confirmed about him.

"Jesus replied, "Let it be so now; it is proper for us to do this to fulfil all righteousness." Then John consented. As soon as Jesus was baptised, he went up out of the water. At that moment heaven was opened and he saw the Spirit of God descending like a dove and lightning on him. And a voice from heaven said, "This is my Son, whom I love; with him I am well pleased" {Matthew3:15-17}

And Jesus himself confirmed that He was the one that was prophesied long time ago to be sent. The coming of Jesus Christ was the fulfilment of the promise that God made to us for our saviour.

"For the Son of Man has come to save that which was lost" {Matthew 18:11}

"For I have come down from heaven not to do my will but the will of him who sent me. And this is the will of him who sent me, that I shall lose none of all that he has given me, but

raise them up at the last day " {John 6:38-39}.

" So Jesus said," When you have lifted up the Son of Man, then you will know that I am [the one I claim to be] and that I do nothing on my own but speak just what the Father has taught me" { John 8:28}

Since He was there, in the beginning He have to come and to rescue His people by bringing up a new law that contains grace and truth.

" For the law was given through Moses, grace and truth came through Jesus Christ" {John 1:17}

Therefore! The law that Jesus Christ brought was the law to set man free from the law of sin and death but take man through the law of Spirit of life.

"Therefore, there is NOW no condemnation for those who are in Christ Jesus. Because through Christ Jesus the law of the Spirit of life set me free from the law of sin and death". {Romans 8:1-2}

Since you are that image of the living God Almighty, let this mind be in you as well, which was also in Christ Jesus; who, being in the form of God, but made himself not to be equal with God, therefore let us die to ourselves, and live a Christ like lives and live a righteous life.

"Your attitude should be the same as that of Christ Jesus: Who being in every nature God, did not consider equality with God something to be grasped; but made himself nothing, taking the very nature of a servant being made in human likeness. And being found in appearance as a man, he humbled himself and became obedient to death, even death on a cross. Therefore, God exalted him to the highest place and gave him the name that is above every name" {Philippians 2:5-9}

So God is so righteous to send us such a humble saviour to come and save us, God's righteousness and love, made him to give up His son for us to have us in return to be pure and sinless.

"But if Christ is in you, your body is dead because of sin, yet your spirit is alive because of righteousness" {Romans 8:10-11}

"For in the Gospel a righteousness from God is revealed, a righteousness that is by faith from first to last, just as it is written:" the righteous will live by faith"
{Roman1:17}

And God is not unfair, not at all, He revealed his righteousness through a number of men in the scriptures, because that's how God operates so that no one can claim that he did not know or was not aware of what he is going to do.So God really showed and revealed it.

"But now a righteousness from God, apart from law, has been made known, to which the law and the Prophets testify" {Romans 3:21-22}

We are the remnant of God that is left in these last days, and we are blessed to live and experience his righteousness and to be His hope in these days. Therefore we have an obligation to purify ourselves and observe his commands , because we are his reserve. He is looking forward on us.

"Yet I reserve seven thousand in Israel-all whose knees have not bowed down to Baal and all whose mouths have not kissed him". {1 Kings 19:18}.

As Gods remnants and remaining hope, we have an obligation and responsibility to come and humble ourselves before him. Yes, we are wounded indeed down in our hearts, but our righteous God is there for us.

"Come let us turn to the Lord, He has torn us to pieces, but he will heal us; he has injured us, but he will bind up our wounds" {Hosea 6:1}

And in reality, life without God is meaningless, there is nothing without Him that we can achieve or overcome. He is the fortress of many, He is the shoulder for many. There is nowhere else where we can find rest and peace and happiness except the Lord God Almighty.

" The Lord is good, a refuge in times of trouble. He cares for those who trust in him" {Nahum 1:7}

"Now all things are of God, who has reconciled us to himself through Jesus Christ, and has given us the ministry of reconciliation. That is that; God was in Christ reconciling the world to Himself, not imputing their trespasses to them and has committed to us the word of reconciliation.". {2 Corinthians 5:18-19}

Can you see that really God Almighty is so righteous and so loving? That He can give up His son, who have not sin, but He ended up having our sins in his shoulders. Who on earth can do such a sacrifice? Except God himself.

"For He made Him who knew no sin to be sin for us, that we might become the righteousness of God in Him". {2 Corinthians 5:21}

His mercy is new every day. To God be the glory.

Our Love Affair with God

Darkness and Light don't mix.

Darkness cannot drive out darkness, only light can do that. Hate and love are the two separate things. Hate cannot drive out Hate. Only Love can do that.

Being deeply loved by someone gives you strength and a sense of belonging. While loving someone deeply gives you courage. It all starts with Love, love that builds character.

"And now these three remain: Faith, Hope and Love. But the greatest of these is Love." {1 Corinthians 13:13)

Love is the single most powerful and necessary component in life. Love is the origin and foundation of all relationships. Every person needs and has the capacity to connect with other people. That connection is a result of bonding.

Bonding is the ultimate emotional connection. You cannot bond with someone without loving, love establishes a reliable base on which bonding can be built on.

While Love, Compassion and Empathy are interactive, they still manifest duality, the lover and the beloved.

The emphasis is on an individual's feelings, not necessary on mutuality.

Bonding on the other hand is a complete fusion of the two. It creates channel between the giver and the receiver. Pre-occupation with your own desires and needs separates you from others.

Bonding that is just an extension of your own needs, is only bonding tighter with yourself. Bonding must be done with discretion and careful consideration with whom or with what you bond with.

Healthy bonding is the union of the two distinct people, with independent personalities who join for higher purpose than satisfying their own needs. Without bonding; no feelings can be truly realised. Even the healthiest and closest relationship may need 'timeout' with respect of each individual's space.

Bonding means connecting; not only feeling for another person, but being attached to one another. Not just a token commitment, but a total devotion.

Bonding is the emotional spine of every relationship. Just take a look at a mother and a child. What makes them to be close to each other? Have you asked yourself what makes a mother, when she is not around her child, feel and sense that something is happening with her child? When the child cries out nonstop, and people would try to make a child to stop, and they fail, but when the mother comes and hold her child to her chest and the child immediately stops crying.

Why?

It's nothing else, but that inner bond between them. Bonding is an affirmation; it gives one the sense of belonging, the sense that "**I Matter**". I am important and significant. It establishes trust, trust in oneself and trust in others. It instils confidence.

Without bonding and nurturing it, we cannot realise it and be ourselves.

Bonding is the foundation of life. Bonding with others' channels of Love, Discipline, Compassion, Endurance and Humility into a constructive rapport, giving relationship an underpinning quality.

The foundation of bonding is different from any ordinary foundation. It doesn't only rest beneath the higher levels of the structure, but encompassed them all. Whereas all other feelings are individual emotions, separate stories of a building and each have a necessary component of experience.

Bonding, channels, integrate and link them all into one. This creates the bedrock upon which the structure of human emotions firmly stands. Bonding is giving all of yourself, not just part of. It is not one emotion, but all of it. Only then can bonding be constructive and everlasting.

An essential component of bonding is its endurance, its ability to withstand challenges and setbacks. Without endurance there is no chance to develop true bonding.

You too!

You can have this bond with God. God want a relationship with you.

Have you ever thought that you can be in a bonding relationship with the Most High God, the source of life Himself?

The creator himself; Yes, you can be in that relationship, just open up the door of your heart.

"Here I am! I stand at the door and knock. If anyone hears my voice and opens the door, I will go in and eat with him, and he with me". {*Revelations 3:20*}

Looking at the above verse. It says, "I will go and eat with him."

Exactly, what does it really mean?

In you, you have your own personal issues that you are involved in. And God is now showing that He is availing Himself if you share your problems with Him; He is there for you.

And when He says: *"And He with me"*

That simple and easily means that you will be enjoying the things of God with Him.

That's what are friends are for, for good times and bad times; it only happens when you open up your heart and believe in Him, just like Abraham the father of faith. He who enjoyed walking with God in all his life because of his belief to God up to the point that he was called God's friend.

"And the scripture was fulfilled that says, "Abraham believed God, and it was credited to him as righteousness, and he was called Gods credited." {James 2:23}

A number of characters that are mentioned in the bible, they have enjoyed sharing some great and awesome relationships with God and they were blessed in a tremendous way.

Even you ! You can have that opportunity and fall in a love affair with God.

All you can do, it's just to come close to Him, and find out the things He likes and don't like. So, as God, He wants us to do that, He is the Lord.

"Let them know that you, whose name is the Lord----that you alone are the Most High over all the earth". {Psalm 83:18}.

When you are in a relationship with someone, you have to get to know who are his friends and enemies.

"For who ever is not against us is for us" {Mark 9:40}

"This is how we know who the children of God are and who the children of the devil are: Anyone who does not do what is right is not a child of God; nor is anyone who does not love his brother" {1 John 3:10}

"This is how you can recognise the Spirit of God: every Spirit that acknowledges that Jesus Christ has come in the flesh is from God. But every spirit that does not acknowledge Jesus is not from God. This is the spirit of the Antichrist, which you have heard is coming and even now is already in the world" {1 John 4: 2-3}

It may seem difficult to fall in a relationship with God, but it is not. All you need to do is just come closer to him and get to know what are the things He likes and his will.

"Therefore, do not be foolish, but understand what the Lord's will is" {Ephesians 5:15-17}

God's friends do the things He likes most as he does always. Just think of your friends. If you will ill treat them and continue to do the irritating and annoying, unpleasant things they don't like, do you think they will continue their friendship? Can you expect a healthy friendship with them?

Even though they will take and do everything to correct you and make you see that your behaviour towards them is not pleasant and you keep on not listening to them and you are not prepared to change. Surely, they will leave you and step out of that friendship with you, up until you come back to your senses. So as with God.

But he gives us more grace. That is why the scripture says:

"God opposes the proud but give grace to the humble". {James 4:6}.

If you want a perfect, happy and pleasant relationship with God, you must do the things he wants and desires. And God's desire is to see us worshiping Him in Spirit and in truth. That's all He wants from us; He doesn't want so much.

"Yet a time is coming and has now come when the true worshippers will worship the Father in spirit and truth, for they are the kind of worshippers the Father seeks. God is spirit,

and his worshippers must worship in spirit and in truth". {John 4:23-24}

As we have said, bonding is giving all of yourself, not just one emotion. But all of it. It is about sacrifice. My friend, when you get into a relationship and you want to see it growing to a higher level and to be the everlasting one, you have to sacrifice certain things that you love for the sake of a relationship and the one you are involving yourself with. When the one that you are involved with, sees what sacrifices and willingness you have shown to change, it is then that he will start to show seriousness in you too.

"Seek the Lord while he may be found; call on him while he is near" {Isaiah 55: 6}

Inside of you, you must burn with the desire and zeal of getting to know him up to the point of knowing his deepest secrets. By doing so, you are digging deep down the things that are in his heart, and preparing to do the things he wants you to do, just like King David son of Jesse.

"I have found David son of Jesse a man after my own heart; he will do everything I want him to do". {Acts 13:22}

When you are in a relationship with God, God will do greater things for you because he has greater plans for those who belongs to him. He is just like any responsible parent. Everything he does, He is always planning for a better future for his kids.

"'For I know the plans I have for you,' "declares the Lord, 'plans to give you hope and a future. Then you will call upon me and come and pray to me, and I will also listen to you. You will seek me and find me when you seek me with all your heart. I will be found by you,' declares the Lord" . *{Jeremiah 29:11-14}*

When you are in a relationship with God. You become something great. People start to call you by honouring titles such as: *"Sir/Madam"*

Why?

Because they are honouring what they see in you, the one you are in a love affair with.

"He then brought them out and asked, 'Sirs, what must I do to be saved'?" *{Acts 16:30}*

Can you see, the very same people who were called prisoners and were not taken seriously, they are now called by respected names. Why? Because they were with God.

God will make you a great respected person among others; He will make your name great and respected among the people around you.

"I will make you into a great nation and I will bless you; I will make your name great, and you will be a blessing. I will bless those who bless you and whoever curses you I will curse" *{Genesis12:2-3}.*

Why?

Due to the love He has for you and the fact that He wants his name to be known through you. And you are in God's heart; that means He has dreams, plans and desires for you and God uses man to display his power to be known.

"For the scripture says to Pharaoh: 'I have raised you up for this very purpose, that I might display my power in you and that my name might be proclaimed in all the earth'". {Romans 9:17}

How can someone become God's friend? Well the Scriptures shows us that there is no other way or any shortcut of getting to God other than Jesus Christ the lamb, who stood up and was given as a ransom sacrifice to save the world, so that those who believe in him may not perish, but may have an everlasting life.

"For there is one God and one mediator between God and men, the man Christ Jesus, who gave himself as a ransom for all men, the testimony given in its proper time". {1Timothy 2:5-6}

"For God did not send his Son into the world to condemn the world but to save the world through him". {John 3:16}

So, you may ask; why we should build our love affair with God through Jesus Christ? A command and an instruction came from up above to us to follow and to put it into practice.

"And the voice from heaven said, "This is my Son, whom I love; with him I am well pleased ". {Matthew 3 :17}.

Surely we should accept that Jesus Christ is the Lord and Saviour, and God, lives in him and him in God?

"Don't you believe that I am in the Father and that the Father is in me" Believe me when I say that I am in the Father and the Father is in me" {John 14:10 -11}.

Is it not so awesome and easy? You do not have to do much in order to be in a relationship with God the Creator.

Accepting Jesus Christ in your life as your Lord and Saviour, you don't just become a friend of God; it goes beyond that, up to the point that you became a child of God.

"Yet to all who received him, to those who believed in his name, he gave the right to be called children of God. Children born not of natural descent, nor of human decision or a husbands will, but born of God, " {John 1:12-13}

Why is a child so much better than a friend? As we have said, between a child and a parent there is a special bonding in them. A child's hope and trust is in his/her parents, in good and in bad times and a parent knows that he/she has a responsibility to look and take care of that child. One of those things or responsibilities of a parent is to provide a shelter for the children.

As much as you should accept Jesus Christ as your Lord. You became a child of God, and when you became a child of God, you shared a home with Jesus. That means you become a brother and a sister to Jesus. That totally means that you have the same privileges as Him.

"For whoever does the will of my Father in heaven is my brother and sister and mother " {Matthew 12:50}

Why?
Because only brothers and sisters can have the same share in their parents' home.

" My Father will love him, and we will come to him and make our home with him" {John 14:23}

In any family. In order to for there to be a peaceful, strong, steady, healthy and trustworthy relationship, there must be communication. Communication is vital to any relationship; there is peace; harmony and understanding among each other and openness to one another. You speak and listen to one another. The only way to communicate with God is through Prayer and Bible reading.

"In addition to all this, take up the shield of faith, with which you can extinguish all the flaming arrows of the evil one. Take the helmet of salvation and the sword of the Spirit, which is the word of God. And pray in the Spirit on all occasions with all kinds of prayers and requests. With this in mind, be alert and always keep on praying for all the saints." {Ephesians 6:17-18}

"Do not be anxious about everything, by prayer and petition, with Thanksgiving, present your requests to God ". {Philippians 4:6}

"All scripture is God breathed and is useful for teaching, rebuking, correcting and training in righteousness, so that the man of God may be thoroughly equipped for every good work." {2 Timothy 3:16}

"Do not let this book of the Law to depart from your mouth, meditate on it day and night, so that you may be careful to do everything written in it. Then you will be prosperous and successful " {Joshua1:8}.

"Behold, I am coming soon! Blessed is he who keeps the words of the prophecy in this book". {Revelations 22:7}

To maintain your relationship with God, you must always be filled with love towards Him. The more you communicate with Him, the more your love grows and your Zeal and Passion of worshipping Him grows inside you.

The only way to show ourselves that we love God, is by obeying His commands and to do His will.

" This is how we know that we love the children of God: by loving God and carrying his commands. This is love for God: to obey his commands and his commands are not burdensome".
{1 John5: 2-3}

If we are in a relationship with God, we must love His people, by loving each other and be there for each other and carry each other's burdens. God's friends don't underestimate others no matter how poor they are or what race they belong to. And as children of God. We should love each other first.

"Let no dept remain outstanding, except the continuing dept to love one another" {Romans 13:8}

"Share with Gods people who are in need. Practice hospitality, (Verse15)

Rejoice with those who rejoice; and mourn with those who mourn. 16, Live in harmony with one another. Do not be proud, but be willing to associate with people of low position. Do not be conceited" {Romans 12:13 & 15-16}

"Let us not become weary in doing good, for at the proper time we will reap a harvest if we do not give up. Therefore, as we have opportunity, let us do good to all people, especially to those who belong to the family of believers" {Galatians6:9-10}

"If anyone says, 'I love God,' yet hates his brother, he is a liar. For anyone who does not love his brother, whom he has seen, cannot love God, whom he has not seen" {1 John 4:20-21}

For the Lord God is a sun and a shield; He gives grace and a glory, no good thing will He withhold from those who walk upright.

"For the Lord God is a sun and a shield; the Lord bestows favour and honour; no good thing does he withhold from those whose walk is blameless. O Lord Almighty blessed is the man who trust in you". {Psalm 84 :11-12}

So, we have to strive and strengthen our love affair with God at all times. There will be things that will try to remove and shift you from your love affair with God.

But you must not even try to entertain those things; as you know, should you even try to leave God for the things of this world, you will be leading your life to destruction and condemnation.

Sin and Man

"And the serpent said to the woman, Ye shall not surely die".
{Genesis 3:4}

When God created a man. He did not create a man to die. But there was a way for a man that will lead him to death. That way was only one way, and that way, its oñly a man that could lead himself to death by eating from the tree of life and death.

The serpent came unto a woman and deceived her by means of misinterpreting what the Lord has said to them. And that is how a man led himself to death by not keeping to what the Lord said to him, instead he listened to the serpent. That very same serpent is still alive and at his work even today; he is busy misleading God's people, Preachers, Priests and Teachers of the word of God.

The devil is still misleading God's people telling them that even if they are saved they won't die, so they can continue to sin. That is the deceit he is busy doing.

So the question is:

Can A Born-Again Person Go to Hell?

When the serpent deceived man, he did not use any energy or strength to lead man to sin, he just played with man's mind , thinking and consciousness.

Because God said:

"Of every tree of the garden you may freely eat; but of the tree of knowledge of good and evil, you shall not eat to it, because the day you eat, surely you will die" {Genesis 2: 16-17}

So the devil worked on man's mind to think that, what God said, He didn't mean it, when He said they will die. Because we see the serpent saying, you shall not surely die, but God really did mean it.

There is nowhere whereby God did not mean whatever He says and whatever God says surely it happens.

"So is my word that goes out from mouth. It will not return to me empty, but will accomplish what I desire and achieve the purpose for which I sent it." {Isaiah 55:11}

Look when He was creating, we saw God in book of {Genesis1:3-29} it is written that *"and God said"*. Can you notice that God, whenever He says there must be something, and whatever *He said* it really happened?

It is no wonder why He even said to them {*Adam & Eve*} that they will die when they ate from that tree. Because He knows that, as God, whatever He says surely it happens. And the serpent was aware of that, but just because he had his own aims and goals to see man drifting away from God, he came with a deceit agenda by just misinterpreting the word of God.

So that is what the devil is still doing even today, devil is still misleading God's people and in these days, he is not coming directly as he did to Eve before, since he knew that we are aware of his past forms and deceit. He is now still using our weak points.

The devil is aware that people are eager for health in their sickness and diseases and also we are running after prosperity, so he used that advantage to mislead us by bringing up pastors that will preach the gospel of prosperity, not repentance.

"Watch out for false prophets, they come to you in sheep's clothing, but inwardly they are ferocious wolves. By their fruit you will recognise them" {Matthew 7:15-16}

That makes us to be careful of the schemes of the serpent the devil so that we will not find ourselves falling to his traps and deception.

"Jesus answered, 'Watched out that no one deceives you. For many will come in my name, claiming, 'I am the Christ, and will deceive many". 24 "For false Christ and false prophets will appear and perform great signs and miracles to deceive even the elect-if that were possible". {Matthew 24:4-5 and 24}.

So the devil-possessed are out there performing wonders claiming they are saved and deceiving people and not living according to the standard that God want. They make people who are around them not see the need and necessity to live a holy upright life. But what God says is:

"Know ye not that the unrighteous shall not inherit the kingdom of God? Be not deceived........". {1 Corinthians 6: 9-10}

What does that really mean? It means that the Heaven is for those who purifies themselves and make themselves Holy. You make yourself blameless before the Lord.

"When a person commits a violation and sins unintentionally in regard to any of the Lords Holy things, he is to bring to the Lord as a penalty a ram from the flock, one without defect and of the proper value". {Leviticus 5:15}

Today we purify ourselves through the blood of our Lord Jesus Christ the lamb, as he was the only lamb that was found blameless in the eyes of God and He himself as He is also a creator. There is no need of slaughtering anything because the blood that fall on the Cross, fell to cleanse us and to wash away our sins.

If Adam and Eve, would have listened to what the Lord have told them, they would not have been fallen into a false deceit of the serpent. So it's so dangerous not to listen to God and keep the words of the Lord. There are outcomes in not listening.

"To obey is better than sacrifice, and to heed, is better than the fat of rams. For rebellion is like the sin of decimation, and arrogance like the evil of idolatry. Because you have rejected the word of the Lord, He has rejected you as king." {1 Samuel 15:22-23}

So that is what happens when you do not listen to God, *God rejects you.* Saul did not listen to the commands of the Lord, when he was commanded to kill and destroy everything.

"Now go, attack the Amalekites and totally destroy everything that belongs to them". {1Samuel 15:3}

Instead he kept some fat ones for burnt offerings; of which offerings don't delight the Lord. What God wants out of us is obedience. Listening and doing as He commands us.

In order to look good in front of the Lord and to go to heaven, we have to kill everything that contaminates us from the Lord.

What is it that you are still keeping in you, that you don't destroy? Whatever it is, you must know that it separates you from God, it is standing as a wall between you and the Lord. *Destroy it!*

Teachers, Prophets, Priests are out there telling people to be saved and be born again, and quote to them that, the scripture says :

"There is no condemnation for those who are in Christ Jesus......". {Romans 8:1}

Yes. That is true. But it doesn't end there. If you go down the verse you will notice that it talks about the way of conduct, it shows us who are exactly those that are not getting condemned.

"Who walk not after the flesh, but after the Spirit."

Therefore, even if you claim you are born again but still live after the desires of the flesh, you will die.

"For if you live according to the flesh you will die ; but if by the Spirit you put to death the misdeeds of the body you will live" . {Romans 8:12-14 }

So what does that mean really when it says 'there is no condemnation for those who are in Christ'? It surely means that those who don't sin and live according to the desires of the flesh, but according to what the Spirit wants are the ones who are not condemned.

"No one, Sir, 'she said. "Then neither do I condemn you," Jesus declared. "Go now and leave your life of sin". {John 8:11}

Jesus here did not condemn this woman; all we can see is that, He told this woman to go and sin no more.

Why to go and sin no more?

Because Jesus knew that her sin is the one that will condemn her. So the devil as we have said is out there still deceiving even the elect, and they will answer to God by not telling the people the truth about God and His righteousness.

"Son of man, I have made you a watchman for the house of Israel; so hear the word I speak and give them warning from me. When I say to a wicked man, 'You will surely die,' and you do not warn him or speak out to dissuade him from his evil ways in order to save his life , that wicked man will die for his sin, and I will hold you accountable for his blood. But if you do warn the wicked man and he does not turn from his wickedness or from his evil ways, he will die for his sin; but you will have saved yourself ". {Ezekiel 3:17-20}.

Some of the preachers of the word of God have turned their backs from the truth of Christ because they want to be loved and to win big numbers for their congregations, they are the people pleasers.

"Am I now trying to win the approval of men, or of God? Or am I trying to please men? If I were still to please men, I would not be a servant of Christ." {Galatians 1:10}

A real man of God who preaches the word of God does not compromise with the truth of God, he preaches it the way it is, and people are still in sin because these things are not said and pin pointed to them, instead pastors do the opposite.

"Preach the Word; be prepared in season and out of season; correct, rebuke and encourage with great patience and careful instruction. For the time will come when men will not put with sound doctrine. Instead, to suit their own desires, they will gather around them a great number of teachers to say what their itching ears want to hear. They will turn their ears away from the truth and turn aside to myths" {2 *Timothy* 4:2-4 }.

Even you who have accepted the Lord Christ Jesus, but not holding to his truth you will be responsible for your deeds, shame on those who lead astray God's people, your end will be the results of your actions. People keep on entertaining false prophets that are leading them to eternal condemnation.

"For such men are false apostles, deceitful workmen, masquerading as the apostles of Christ. And no wonder for Satan himself masquerades as an angel of light. It is not surprising, then, if his servants masquerade as servants of

righteousness. Their end will be what their actions deserve". {2 Corinth 11:13-15}.

People are turning away from the true gospel of Christ, running after the false doctrines.

"I am astonished that you so quickly deserting the one who called you by the grace of Christ and are turning to a different gospel, which is really no gospel at all. Evidently some people are throwing you into confusion". {Galatians 1:6-9}.

And if we knew that, in life, in this world we are living in. There is no external power that can separate us from the Lord; however; we can separate ourselves from God through sin. Sin is an ugly and unaccepted thing to God; Righteousness never hides Gods face from you; but Sin does and God won't hear your prayers If you sin.

"You must know that your iniquities separate you from God." {Isaiah 59:2}

And what the Lord is saying its very simple and straight forward that There must not be even a HINT of sin.

"But among you there must not be even a <u>hint</u> of sexual immorality, or of any kind of impurity, or of greed, because these are improper for Gods holy people" {Ephesians 5:3-6},

And God made it totally clear and straight forward of what He wants out of us.

" For it is written, "Be holy, because I am holy ". {1 Peter 1:16 }

Can you see, we people like to take things for granted, saying no its just a minor, a once off thing. It will just pass, forgotten that people get addicted in their lives to what they thought it was nothing much at the beginning. It is no wonder God says that there must not be even a Hint.

WHY? Take a typical example of a big white clean cloth sheet hanging on the wall and in that cloth, there is a little stain of a drop as small as the grain of rice.

Where do you think will be the eyes of those who are looking at that sheet mostly? Will not their eyes and attention be on that little stain that is there?

Surely their focus will be looking on that stain.

They will even say, "Yes, we see that the cloth is clean and white, but there is a stain on it. " Because God knows the outcome of ignorance.

So tell me. How can you have fellowship with God, while you walk in darkness?

Can you give me a sincere answer to this question?

There is no way, just as you were born of the Spirit of God, you can lose your salvation, and turn from the light, back into darkness, you are lost as far as God is concerned; you are back in darkness of sin.

Prayers won't make you see God. Fasting won't make you see God. Singing won't make you see God. Evangelism won't make you see God. Being a worker won't make you see God. Attending Church regularly won't make you see God either. You can preach and preach, but won't make you see God.

Only a life of Holiness alone, that can make you see God, for God is Holy, it is no wonder we are told that it is those who have clean hands and pure heart who will stand in God's presence.

" Who may ascend the hill of the Lord?
Who may stand in his holy place?
He who has clean hands

and a pure heart,
who does not lift up his soul
to an idol. " {Psalms 24:3-4}

Serving God is rewarding. Only when you serve God in purity. Not serving God in sin. Without Holiness, no one can see the Lord.

"For it is written: 'Be holy, because I am holy." {1 Peter 1: 16}

" *I am the Lord your God, consecrate yourselves and .be holy, because I am holy. Do not make yourselves unclean by any creature that moves about on the ground."* {Leviticus 11: 44}

A lot is said and has been shown by the word of God. But people are deaf to hear and blind to see what the word of God is teaching them.

"For these people's heart has become calloused; they hardly hear with their ears, and they have closed their eyes". *{Matthew 13:15} .*

The sad and pitiful part to all of this is, people who are in this are those who are church members without any God in them, yet claiming to have eternal life because false doctrine has been preached strongly to them. And because of a lot of information they have in them, and they know the scriptures they even now have a sweet way of indulging themselves to sin, and in scriptures they choose what is good and pleasing for themselves.

"And He said to them: You have a fine way of setting aside the commands of God in order to observe your own traditions" *{Mark 7:9}*

So that takes us back to the question we have before: Can a born-again person go to hell???

What the scriptures says:

"Not everyone who says to me, Lord, Lord, will enter the Kingdom of Heaven, but only he who does the will of my father in heaven" . {Matthew 7:21}

" For I tell you that unless your righteousness surpasses that of the law, you will certainly not enter the kingdom of heaven". {Matthew 5:20}

So if you cannot enter the kingdom of heaven, that means you will go to hell, because its either hell or heaven, there is no middle place.

Therefore! If you cannot enter heaven, that shows that you don't belong to the Father who is in heaven; if you don't belong to Him, that will mean you have another father, so that father if it cannot be God, surely it is the devil. Why the devil?

Because in the scriptures there are only two fathers that are mentioned, it is Father God and father the devil.

"You belong to your father the devil, and you want to carry out your father's desires. He was a murder from the beginning, not holding to the truth, for there is no truth in him" {John8:44}

Then if you belong to the devil, surely you will not enter the kingdom of heaven. Sin stands as a wall between man and God.

So don't just claim to be a saved born-again person , but knowing deep down that you are still doing unacceptable and unpleasant things to the eyes of the father in heaven. Repent and live your life for God. Stop sinning and come back to the Lord God Almighty and hold on to his teachings and live by his Spirit.

"The Spirit gives life; the flesh counts for nothing. The words I have spoken to you are spirit and they are life". {John 6:63}.

So a man has to live by the Spirit in order to get rid of the sin and live a pleasing life for God. Because that is the kind of worshipers God want to see.

"Yet a time is coming and has now come when the true worshippers will worship the Father in Spirit and truth, for they are the kind of worshippers the Father seek. God is spirit, and his worshippers must worship in spirit and in truth" {John 4:23}

Crucify the flesh

Very few of us who seem to be aware of the fight to death conflict Christians are in with their sinful nature of flesh. Christians are faced with a big and challenging battle in them. That battle is caused by the flesh its self. The flesh has a number of desires that lead the children of God to the point that he/her ends up sinning, doing the things he/she supposed not to do.

The things that are totally against the will of God, because they are sin. We are all aware that sin separates man from God and sin will lead you to eternal condemnation.

In order to avoid this, anyone who claims to be the child of God and wants to live an everlasting eternal life with God our creator in heaven, you have to deal with the desires of your body and fight them.

The only way to do so is through crucifying the desires of the body because the devil is using the body to lead you to sin.

How can you crucify those desires? By resisting. When resisting is when you say no to the desires of the flesh, and not allowing them in your life to control you. Should you not let them to control you, the devil will flee from you.

"Submit yourselves then to God, resist the devil, and he will flee from you"

{James 4:7-10}

Therefore; the only way of resisting the devil is through crucifying the body. What is this crucifixion?

Crucifixion is a form of a slow and painful execution that was used to punish the one who has done something wrong. That person was tied and nailed to a large wooden cross and that person was left to hang there until he dies.

It is no wonder why we hear Jesus say we must be prepared to lay down our lives for Him.

"If anyone comes to me and does not hate his Father and Mother, his wife and children, his brothers and sisters - yes even his own life -- he cannot be my disciple. And anyone who does not carry the cross and follow me cannot be my disciple."

{Luke1 4:26-27}

Why He said so; because He knew that when laying down our lives, we will not be gratified by the desires of the sinful nature that will lead us to death so when you crucify your flesh; that means you lay down and kill its desires.

Why He spoke of carrying the cross?

Jesus was giving this example of the cross, because he knows how the cross weighs. It was something that was difficult and heavy to carry. The victim was asked to carry it up to the place of its crucifixion and while he was carrying it, he was feeling the pain of the weight of the cross. It was used to hang anyone who is execute; in other words, he was saying that to follow him, you must execute the desires of your body.

Yes! It won't be something easy and comfortable to see yourself suffering, but you will be doing that for the best things to come and with the hope that you will be with Jesus Christ where He is. That is the positive attitude of any Christian to live and Hope for.

"For in this hope we were saved. But hope that is seen is no hope at all. Who hope for what he already has? But if we hope for what we do not yet have, we wait for it patiently " {Romans 8:24-25}

So when you are waiting patiently, you guard and watch your steps, you don't just do as the others do, because you may spoil and miss the opportunities of getting what you have been longing for. Which means that, we have to purify ourselves and live a holy upright life.

"Since we have these promises, dear friends, let us purify ourselves from everything that contaminates body and spirit, perfecting holiness out of reverence for God." {2 Corinthians 7:1}

Let us purify; "**Purify** ". What is needed and expected out of us is to live a pure life, the blameless one, the only way that can make any Christian to live the life that God wants is to live by the Spirit.

"So I say, live by the Spirit, and you will not gratify the desires of the sinful nature. For the sinful nature desires what is contrary to the Spirit, and the Spirit what is contrary to the sinful nature. They are in conflict with each other, so that you do not do what you want. But if you are led by the Spirit, you are not under law." {Galatians 5:16-18}

What does it really mean when it says they are in conflict with each other?

It really means that you can't claim living in Spirit while on the other hand you are busy in sin. It won't work, actually it doesn't work like that at all. When you live the desires of the sinful nature, you let your body do the things that you yourself want. When you think deep down in your consciousness they don't make you happy at all, that is the conflict that we are talking about; that the Spirit and sin are in conflict with each other.

"I do not understand what I do. For what I want to do I do not do, but what I hate, I do. 17 " As it is, it is no longer I myself who do it, but it is sin living in me." {Romans 7 :15&17}

Can you see what the sin does to man, can you see what conflict that it creates And surely when there is a conflict, there would be some consequences and the end results of that conflict, well if it is so, that you see yourself doing the things you don't want to do, surely there is a problem.

"The one who sows to please his sinful nature, from that nature' will reap destruction; the one who sows to please the Spirit will reap eternal life." {Galatians 6 :7-8}

Sin is working in three phases in a humankind. Body, Soul and the Spirit. Let us see how the sin works in these three phases.

Body

"What a wretched man I am! Who can rescue me from this body of death?"
{Romans 7:24}

"Therefore, God gave them over in the sin desires of their hearts to sexual impurities for the degrading of their bodies with one another." {Romans 1:24}

When you allow your body to sexual immorality, lust. God don't work with a person who is involved in sexual immorality. The devil has deceived many who think sexual immorality is all right. It is even now brought forward and is shown on televisions so that people can recognise and accept it and think it is right.

Even the people who are involved in it, they misinterpret the word of God to fulfil their dirty desires. But to God it is not acceptable.

Soul

"The heart is deceitful, above all things and beyond cure. Who can understand it? I the Lord search the heart and examine *the mind, to reward a man according to his conducts, according to what his deeds deserve."* {Jeremiah 17 :9-10}

"Because the sinful mind is hostile to God. It does not submit to God's laws, nor can it do so." {Romans 8:7 }

"But now you rid yourselves of all such things as these: Anger, range, malice, slander and filthy language in your lips. Do not lie to each other, since you have taken off your old self with its practices." {Colossians 3:8-9}

Others in their hearts are not forgiving, they hold grudges in them. Yes! We admit that they have wronged and hurt you a lot, but you must forget and forgive them. Don't hold prisoners in your heart, because that will haunt you. Your soul will be affected. If you do not forgive them, God will not forgive you too.

Spirit

"Or do you think Scriptures says without reason that the Spirit He caused to live in us envies intensely?" {James 4:5}

"Watch and pray so that you will not fall into temptation. The spirit is Willing, but the body is weak." {Matthew 26:41}

The spirit suffers and struggle to function when the body is in sin, it makes it even difficult to pray because the spirit is depressed.

Can you see how the sin works in a human being. It causes a great big damage. It makes the whole of a human being dirty in the eyes of the Lord God Almighty. Can you see that we really need to live a blameless pure life so that when Jesus comes back, he will find us in a right position and if any of these three phases' is affected in sin; that shows that God is not happy with you.

"May your whole spirit, soul, and body be kept blameless at the coming of our Lord Jesus Christ". {1 Thessalonians 5:23}

Surely there are things that make these three phases to be affected. The things we do, we see and we think make us sin, but the question may come, how can we avoid such things; what does the Scripture say?

"If your right eye causes you to sin, gouge it out and throw it away", and if your right hand causes you to sin, cut it off and throw it away. It is better for you to lose one part of your body than for your whole body to go into hell." {Matthew 5:29-30}

Why is there a need for you to gouge out the eye specifically?

It is all because everything that a person does starts within the eye. Should you see something with your eye, it will send a massage straightforward to your brain that will start working in your mind. When it is working in your mind, your soul start getting affected and when your soul start getting affected your spirit becomes involved and affected. When it is affected you start to think of doing or putting into practice what you have seen and cravings develop and your body gets involved.

It is then that you get yourself in sin. In other words, you become full of desires of doing it. If you care to remember Eve, when she saw the fruit that it was good, she grew desires for it and ate at the tree.

"So when the woman saw that the tree was good for food, that it was pleasant to the eyes, and a tree desirable to make one wise, she took of its fruit and ate. She also gave to her husband with her, and he ate". {*Genesis 3:6*}

Can you see the devil will show you things that when you set your eyes on it, they will look good and pleasant to you, unaware that they are your pitfall?

"The eye is the lamp of the body, if your eyes are good, your whole body will be full of light. But if your eyes are bad, your whole body will be full of darkness. If then the light within you is darkness, how great is that darkness." {Matthew 6:22-23}

So if your eyes were in the light, you will not fall into the pit of the deceit of the devils schemes. You will be aware of him at all times. People are involved in sexual immorality, lust, stealing, drugs.

"Do you not know that your body is a temple of the Holy Spirit, who is in you, whom you have received from God? You are not your own; You were bought at a price. Therefore, honour God with your body" {1Corinthiàns 6:19-20}

Well if it is so, that you find yourself doing the things you don't want to do, surely there is a problem.

"I do not understand what I do. For what I want to do I do not do, but what I hate I do, and if I do what I do not want to do, I agree that the law is good. As it is, it is no longer I who do it, but it is sin living in me. I know that nothing good lives in me, that is, in my sinful nature. For I have the desire to do what is good, but I cannot carry it out. For what I do is not the

good I want to do; no, the evil I do not want to do---this I keep on doing. Now if I do what I do not want to do, it is no longer I who do it, but it is sin living in me that does it. So I find this law at work: When I want to do good, evil is right there with me. For in my inner being I delight in God's law; but I see another law at work in the members of my body, waging war against the law of my mind and making me a prisoner of the law of sin at work within my members. What a wretched man I am! Who will rescue me from this body of death?" {Romans 7:15-24}

But in Christ Jesus my Lord, there is a solution and a way out to whatever the situation is with your life. As the scripture say:

"Humble yourselves, therefore, under Gods mighty hand, that he may lift you up in due time. Cast all your anxiety on him because he cares for you." {1 Peter 5:6-7}

So make a choice with your life make a decided now. There are personal choices and decisions that each and every single individual must take in order to follow to a direction that you desire. Also, in life there are two roads that a man can take. One leads to life, the other leads to death and destruction.

There is no middle or a short cut road. So it is all up to you, God won't make decisions for you on how you can live your life. But thanks God, we serve an awesome God, who gives us choices. Therefore, God has given us an offer of life and death, it's all up to us:

"This day, I call heaven and earth as witnesses against you that I have set before your Life and Death, blessings and curses. Now choose life, so that you and your children may live." {Deuteronomy 30:19 }

So choose wisely and crucify the flesh and get rid of its desires. If you want to see abundances in your life, then put sin out of your life and live a self-controlled life.

"That each of you should learn to control his own body in a way that is holy and honourable" {1 Thessalonians 4:1-4}.

So scriptures are clear. The only way to have a closer relationship with God and to live a life of abundance in Christ Jesus, is to stop sinning and crucify the flesh. In fact; there is a very unpopular concept that we must think of very soberly.

We must prove ourselves to God. We must demonstrate our obedience and faith. Jesus learned obedience through suffering.

Can we do any less or more for our God? The hard facts are these, we cannot progress in our growth in the Lord without first proving ourselves obedient and faithful to God by putting sin out of our lives.

"For the grace of God that brings salvation has appeared to all men. It teaches us to say "No" to ungodliness and worldly passions and to live self-controlled, upright and godly lives in this present age." {Titus 2: 11-14}

You will not grow or improve yourself as long as you continue to allow active sin in your life. God so intensely desires us to be cleansed from sin that he gave up His very own life to provide for our purification.

We too also, we must intensely desire to be free from sin that we are willing to lay down anything to crucify the flesh and its desires, no matter how painful it may be, but we have to suffer for our salvation by getting rid of sin in our bodies.

So how can we have victory in this struggle against our sin nature? The answer is simple. We must acquire more power than our sin nature has; or we can never overcome it. Where can we get that power? The answer is simple:

"Have nothing to do with the fruitless deeds of darkness, but rather expose them." {**Ephesians** 5:11-13 }

You know what, the devil likes to hide in a man by making a man to feel ashamed of mentioning what he is doing in secret. In that way a man keeps on sinning If you distance yourself from the things that contaminates you to what the Lord want out of you and if you expose the sin, and confess your sins , when the devil seeing that you are exposing and resisting him and his deeds, he will surely flee from you. The only way that can give you strength and courage to do that is to be submissive to the Lord God.

"Submit yourselves then to God. Resist the devil and he will flee from you."
{James 4:7-10}

If we will obey what the word of God is commanding us to do, and to have a self-controlled life. Also live our lives to please the Lord, basically it is not about pleasing the Lord God. It's about preparing our future life; that is Eternal life, so it's up to you, where do you want to spend your eternity, in hell or Heaven? If you want to see yourself in heaven. You have to crucify the flesh and get rid of the sins that are corrupting you and separating your relationship with your creator.

Grow in the Lord

Are you one of those who says:

"I will never get anything out of the messages at church, they don't make any change in my Spiritual life."

If that is you who says this, this may not be the fault of the person who is preaching. It could be the way you are hearing. It might have to do with whether or not you are opening up your heart and really desiring to know those truths.

"Blessed are those who hunger and thirst for righteousness, for they will be filled." {Matthew 5:6}

Does this describe you? The way you view things?

If so, well then that describes you with the level you are in it in your spiritual growth. If you get to where you want to grow in the Lord, the truth of God's Word, more than you crave food, more than you desire wealth, you will get it.

The problem is that most of us only want this every once in a while. Maybe once in a week or month, we have a little twinge of desire of growth for five or ten minutes where we would like to understand and be operating in more spirituality, but then we get occupied with everything else in life and that desire of growth fades. If that's the way you are, you will never ever going to have this understanding.

God is not the one who determines the condition of your growth. You are the one.

It basically just boils down to where your focus is. If you are focused on the Lord, and you are hungry and seeking for growth in Him, you will be filled. But if you are not the one depicted in this parable, the word of God just doesn't mean anything to you.

You can hear it, and it's gone before you even think about it. You just can't seem to retain God's word. Is it not time for you to pray and ask God to speak louder to you? Is it not time for you to change your heart and start focusing on the things of the Lord in order to gain growth ?

Let me make another statement: This parable also describes progressive steps towards fruitfulness in growth.

The Lord here clearly describes four different types of people's hearts, and how the word of God interacts within their hearts to bring forth fruits of growth in them. Jesus was describing four different stages towards growth.

First you go through a stage where you hear the word of God, but your heart is not set on it. You are not seeking after the things of God; the word goes to one ear and goes out to another.

(1) " *Other seed fell among thorns, which grew up and chocked the plants; so that they did not bear grain"* {Mark 4:7}

Jesus talks about this second type of person that hear the word of God. But as they heard it, it is not deeply rooted in their hearts, when challenges come, and toss them back and front, they easily desert the Lord.

(2) " *Others, like seed sown on rocky places, hear the word and at once receive it with joy. But since they have no root, they last only a short time. When trouble or persecutions comes because of the word, they quickly fall away."* {Mark 4:16-17}

To the third type, the word of God begins to germinate and start producing life in them, but then they get distracted by the things of this world. When those distractions come, their growth fades away.

(3) " Still others, like seed sown among thorns, hear the word; but the worries of this life, the deceitfulness of wealth and the desires for other things come in and choke the word, making it unfruitful " {Mark 4:18-19}

The fourth type of a person is the one who really natures and takes care of the Word of God. They focus on it and are not distracted by the things of this world, so they produce good fruits of growth out of it.

* *(4) Others, like seed sown on good soil, hear the word, accept it, and produce a crop ---thirty, sixty or even a hundred times what was sown." {Mark 4:20}*

Through my experiences, I have learned a lesson that: A seed must first of all grow underground; when it is underground it may seem as if it is finished dead and buried. When you dig it where it is buried, you will discover that it is rotten. No, it is not. It is where its life is starting, because as it is under ground. It is where it will start to grow roots; after that it will germinate above the ground as a small tree.

A tree with strong roots will grow up high under all the good and bad circumstances of nature around it, the outcomes of standing those circumstances it will produce fruits.

In the spiritual realm, many people don't like the root stage. They don't like a truth from the Word of God to root inside of them and get established in their hearts.

They just want to skip all this and get right to the fruit stage/level as quickly as they can. Therefore, they don't have very much depth in their life. Their heart is not totally committed to the truth they have received. They may look like they are growing faster than anybody else; but in the end, they can't sustain their growth.

They shrivelled up and died at the first little hardship that comes along. The Word is not producing fruits in their lives. If you want to be someone who really produces fruits and sees the word of God doing its work on you, it's not just going to happen overnight. You can't just jump to your miracle growth. It takes persistence.

You have to let the word of the Lord God to stay rooted inside you. You have to keep on digging and looking for greater revelations. Should you fail to let the word of God dwell and be rooted inside of you. That would be the number one reason why you won't see greater fruits in your spiritual life and manifestation of growth in you because you have not given the word of God some time.

So when are you going to open up your heart to the word of the Lord to do its work in you?

If it is not **now,** when? When will **'Now'** be? The now that is this moment, never existed before and will never exist again.

Therefore, one must keep in mind, that every '**Now'** has its own special time and function.

"Now" is the only time you own, live, love, and toil.

See every moment as a new '**Now'** with its potential and that it will never come back.

The next moment has its own mission. If we waste a '**Now'**-- when can we ever make up that loss?

We must distinguish between what is major and what is relatively minor, because otherwise we may spend our time on trivia and neglect major items. If the big things are taken care of at first, you may as well be able to get everything done.

What you want to dream, that is the beauty of the human mind. To do anything that you want to do, that is the strength of the mans will. To trust yourself, to test your limits, that is the courage to succeed.

"There is a time for everything, and a season for every activity under heaven."
{Ecclesiastes 3:1}

Therefore, there is no way that someone can stay and remain in one place if you have those things within you. Each and every single individual is not expected to remain in one place, but to grow, as much as in the Lord. We have to grow as the time goes by. From one level to the next level.

But the problem we are faced with is; we the children of God, is that there are some who don't want to grow in the Lord spiritually. They still need to be spoon-fed.

They still behave and act like kids in the house of the Lord. God wants to do and to reveal himself to them in different ways, but God cannot do that because He still sees that people are not yet ready to experience more things of heaven.

"For though by this time you ought to be teachers, you need someone to teach you again the first principles of the oracles of God; and you have come to need milk and not solid food. For everyone who partakes only of milk is unskilled in the word of righteousness, for he is a baby. But solid food belongs to those who are of full age, that is those who by reason of use have their sense exercised to discern both good and evil." {Hebrews 5: 12-14}

Who are those of full age that verse 14 is talking about? Those are the ones who are ready and prepared to take rebuke and correction when it comes. That makes them to be given solid food; solid food is for the mature spiritual man. So, the infants when they are rebuked, they get hurt and want to live the house of the Lord.

"Brothers, I could not address you as spiritual, but as worldly, infants in Christ. I gave you milk not solid food, for you were not yet ready for it. Indeed, you are still not ready." {1 Corinthians 3:1-2}

The infants don't have godly sorrow when they are rebuked; they are filled with worldly sorrow, unrepented heart. When the devil gets the heart, the heart without God's feelings, it only has human feelings or that of the devil.

They even come up with excuses that they are weak. That's why they keep on sinning and not growing. That makes it difficult for them to grow. They get stuck in one level in their faith of which that makes them to be in danger of abandoning their faith altogether; because they are not yet ready for solid food.

In the house of the Lord. There are different stages of spirituality and maturity growth. Here we see John addressing the church in three different stages: Children, Young man, & Fathers.

That clearly shows us that in the church people do grow. He addressed them as:

Firstly - Children: Because they are still young to the Lord, now, since they gave themselves up and their sins have been forgiven. They still need to be thought the true elementary teachings about how to be a true and real Christian in the house of the Lord.

They need to be sat down with them. The children are the kind of people here in life that believe in tangible touchable things. They mostly believe to what they see than what they hear. 'Monkey see, Monkey do'. Children possess that character.

Secondly: John described this type of the stage as a stage of **Young man**. At this stage, they can do practical things and theorise. That shows that these young men, they were children before, but as the time goes by, they have grown up to a stage of not being children anymore, but young man and they proved that they have managed to overcome certain obstacles of the evil one.

That thing alone shows that they have grown up they are no longer children any more. What made them to grow is that they have hold on to the word of the Lord and put it into practice and the word was rooted in them, even then, in that situation, they still need to be monitored.

Thirdly: To you **Fathers**. Talking about fathers, we are talking about the adult matured people. Matured people, they just listen to theory and take that theory to practicality.

John shows us that at this stage they are in it now as fathers, they have a lot of experience in knowing the Lord and how they have to conduct themselves and what is their duties and responsibilities are as adults.

Out of them they are the ones who should be the living example to the young ones in the Lord on how to conduct and live in the Lord.

"I write to you, dear children because your sins have been forgiven on account of his name. (13): I write to you, fathers, because you have known him who is from the beginning. I write to you, young men, because you have overcome the evil one. I write to you dear because you have known the Father. (14) I write to you, fathers, because you have known him who is from the beginning. I write to you, young men, because you are strong, and the word of God lives in you, and you have overcome the evil one." {1 John 2:12-14}.

That's what happens when you are in Christ and live in the word of God and meditate on it day and night. You grow from one level of faith and maturity in the Lord. When you have grown up, you get up to the point of knowing Him, you grow in strength of standing the test of times and you grow and became an overcomer.

"But when perfection comes, the imperfect disappears." {1 Corinthians 13:10}

When you have given and accepted the Lord Jesus Christ in your life as your saviour and Redeemer, you will no longer live the life, or let me say, live the life style you used to live before. You completely change, because the life you are living now no longer belongs to you but is of Christ Jesus.

"Therefore, if anyone is in Christ, he is a new creation; the old has gone, the new has come." {2 Corinthians 5:17}

So when you are in the Lord, you will have to change, to discipline yourself in knowing what is right and wrong what to do and not.

"When I was a child, I talked like a child, I thought like a child, I reasoned like a child. When I became a man, I put childish ways behind me." {1 Corinthians 13:11}

You don't think and live according to the standard of this world, you grow in the Lord and get rid of the things of this world, because you no longer of this world.

"Get rid of the old yeast that you may be a new batch without yeast---as you really are. For Christ, our Passover lamb, has been sacrificed." {1 Corinthians 5:7}

We are to come to Christ and lean on Him, taking upon ourselves the growth in him through his yoke, and the results will be a mind informed with divine wisdom, sensitive to all the truth watchful against all evil.

The growth of the outer life depends entirely upon the growth of the inner life, that is the growth in the mind. A man's outward actions for good or bad are all but the fruits of his inner life, thoughts and desires.

" You, however, did not come to know Christ that way. Surely you heard of him and were taught in him in accordance with the truth that is in Jesus. You were taught in regard to your former way of life, to put off your old self which is being corrupted by its deceitful desires. To be made new in the attitude of your minds, and to put on the new self, created to

be like God in true righteousness and holiness." *{Ephesians 4:20-24}*

Now the Christian, who has been given a new heart and a new nature, must appreciate the gift by turning his mind and directing his attentions to the things of Christ, and away from the things of evil. When you have set your mind to the things of the Lord God Almighty, you grow and became rooted in the Lord. When you are rooted in the Lord. You are unshakable you grow stronger and stronger in knowing the Lord.

"So then, just as you received Christ Jesus as Lord, continue to live in him, rooted and built up in him, strengthened in the faith as you were taught, and overflowing with thankfulness." {Colossians 2:6-7}

"For you were once darkness, but now you are light in the Lord. Live as children of light. For the fruit of the light consist in all goodness, righteousness and truth. and find out what pleases the Lord." *{Ephesians 5:8-10}*

"Remember your creator in the days of your youth, before the days of trouble come and the years approach when you will say, "I find no pleasure in them" {Ecclesiastes 12:1}.

Discover Yourself

When God created man on earth, He said: **And let him rule over the earth.** So what was the real purpose of making man? Is the man fulfilling that purpose?

To discover yourself is to have a full knowledge about yourself of who you are, where you come from, and why you are living and what is the purpose. If you look at Paul. We saw Paul saying that as for him, to live is Christ to die is gain.

Why Paul was saying that?

Paul, when he looked at himself, he discovered that there was a man who went to the cross died and rise up for him so that he may be saved from the wrath of the Lord and have an everlasting life.

So to Paul, he felt that Jesus' death was the reason for him to be still alive. So he saw that, since Jesus went on the cross for Him so that he may be alive, he saw that the life he is living now, he is not living it for himself but for the Lord, because the Lord is the reason for him to be alive, He discovered that he is no longer living his own life but the life for the Lord. That is the attitude that you too should have if you have discovered yourself that the reason why you are still alive; it's because of Christ death.

"For to me to live is Christ and to die is gain." {Philippians 1:21}

If you have discovered yourself that Christ is the reason for you to be alive, and that you know where you come from, and that you are the creation of the Lord and Christ is in the Lord God Almighty and if you are in Christ you are in the Lord God, because if you have seen Christ, you have seen the God the father your creator because the father God is in him the two are in one.

" Don't you believe that I am in the Father, and that the Father is in me?" {John 14 :10-11}

And if you have discovered that, you will know that, you have the duty and the responsibility to accomplish on earth. Among us or let me put it this way, in our living communities and wherever we are.

We are surrounded by different kinds and types of people with their different types of issues, challenges, ups and downs, and when these people look at you as a Christian, they see their **Hope.**

They see someone they can turn to for their solutions in their problems. Off which that's our responsibility. We have to make a difference where we are, a Christian in the Lord is a **Salt.**

A salt is what makes food to have a taste. Just have an imagination of a food without salt; surely that food will be tasteless. It won't be enjoyable. You will lose appetite and no interest of continuing to eat it.

So as you; people must have that zeal of being around you, because there is this special thing in you that attracts them.

"You are the salt of the earth. But if the salt loses its saltness, how can it be made salty again? It's no longer good for anything, except to be thrown out and trampled by men." {*Matthew 5:13*} & {*Matthew 9:50*}

That is where now; you as a Christian, you start to get involved in the lives of the hopeless, of those who see things as if they are deem, you come in and bring light to their lives, so they can see that, in whatever they are encountering in their lives, there is future hope for them.

I suggest that you can view yourself as being a **Light.** I mean someone who have a capacity to make darkness disappear, because, you really, you are that person in Christ Jesus. You are the Carrier of the light.

You must radiate this light wherever you go and you are able to help yourself and others to step over the darkness. That light you are, is the positive attitude in you, that brings out hope in everything you come across with because of Christ Jesus that is in you.

"You are the light of the world. A city on a hill cannot be hidden. Neither do people light a lamp and put it under a bowl. Instead they put it on its stand, and it gives light to everyone in the house." {*Matthew5:14-15*}

When you introduce light into a dark area, the darkness just disappears. If you enter a dark place, with a lamp, the light falls on everyone who is in there near you.

You don't have to tell people that there is light. It automatically happens and everyone becomes aware of it, and darkness disappears. That lightness is nothing else, but the things that you do for others, those things that developed hope to the others around you.

If you approach someone, who is experiencing a darkness, with thoughts of fear and the greatness of pain in them, what you just have to do is to identify the darkness.

It may seem to be improper to comfort those in darkness by putting yourself in someone's shoes, but you will help in eliminating that darkness altogether by bringing light to the present moment.

That is what is expected out of you, wherever you go. People around you they must see Jesus Christ in you and when you bring light to darkness, you are bringing an attitude of openness that does not allow truth to be hidden.

Remember: "**Truth shall set you free.**"

Stay in truth. You will truly see the freedom of being in light when you stay in truth, and allow the truth in all that you encounter to take its place. That truth is Jesus Christ, and wherever there is Jesus Christ, there is hope. Without Him, Jesus Christ, our life is deemed.

"In the same way, let your light shine before men, that they may see your good deeds and praise your Father in heaven." {*Matthew 5:16*}

Even Jesus Christ the Lord, knew who He was. Remember He said, I am the Way, Life and the Truth. Jesus said this because he discovered himself of who He is. So Jesus said this also to us, so we may know who we are.

"Jesus answers, 'I am the way and the truth and the life. No one comes to the Father except through me.'" {*John 14:6*}

"Praise be to God and the Father of our Lord Jesus Christ, the Father of compassion and the God of all comfort, who comforts us in all our troubles, so that we can comfort those who are in any trouble with the comfort we ourselves have received from God. For just as the sufferings of Christ flow over into our lives, so also through Christ our comfort overflows. If we are distressed, it is for your comfort, which produces in you patient endurance of the same sufferings we suffer. And our hope for you is firm, because we know that just you share in our sufferings, so also you share in our comfort." {*2 Corinthians 1: 3-7*}

So when you have discovered yourself of who you are, that you are the salt and light to others, that will mean you bring hope and joy to them.

So what is Hope?

It is a feeling of expecting things to go well {optimism}, a thought that says things will improve, things will go in a positive way for me. It won't be always be miserably, dark; there is always a way to rise above the present terrible circumstances.

Hope is an internal awareness that you do not have to suffer forever, and that somehow, somewhere there is a remedy in feeling hopeless {Despair}. That you will come upon if you can only maintain this expectancy in your heart. For it is in the presence of a hopeful vision that hopelessness and suffering no longer hold our attention.

"We know that the whole creation has been groaning as in the pains of childbirth right up to this present time. Not only so, but we ourselves, who have the first fruits of the Spirit, groan inwardly as we wait eagerly for our adoption as sons, the redemption of our bodies. For in this hope we were saved. But hope that is seen is no hope at all. Who hopes for what he already has? But if we hope for what we do not yet have, we wait for it patiently." {Romans 8: 22-25}

Hopelessness is an attitude experienced in the mind. It is the way of looking at a life situation and feeling hopeless. There is no hopelessness in this world. There are only people who are thinking negative. This is a serious point to understand. There may be many upsetting circumstances that may have occurred in your life and in the lives of others yet in and of themselves they are just plain circumstances; those are the facts of life.

Hopelessness itself is a mental process that sizes up and views situations as awful.

When you recognise hopelessness as being a mental attitude you begin a process of bringing hope to the inner vision of despair and dissolving it. It is impossible for hope and despair to exist together at the same time.

One must fail and the other must take place. Most of the time it is despair that usually takes over and cancels out hope. So people who live with an attitude of despair, they never allow themselves to speed up and experience the faster higher frequencies which lead all the way to spiritual energy. Instead they fuel their low and slow energy by processing almost every event from a negative point of view.

As soon as you identify yourself with terms such as "Life is difficult", well that is what you are going to experience in your life. As you think, so shall you be. People who are in the truth of the Lord God, are not selfish, self-centred. They are not only thinking about themselves only and want to see good things only happening to them. They always consider others better than themselves and they know that in order for them to be that salt and light that God want them to be, they must possess the desires to do good things for others.

"Nobody should seek his own good, but the good of others." {1 Corinthians 10:24}

So whatever you do, you shouldn't forget that as a Christian, there is a great commission that was given to you to go and win the souls. Remember what the Lord said to His disciples, to go and make disciples of all the nations and teach them everything He have told them.

"Therefore, go and make disciples of all the nations, baptising them in the name of the Father and of the Son and of the Holy Spirit, and teaching them to obey everything I have commanded you. And surely, I am with you always, to the very end of the age." {Matthew 28:19-20 }

For you to win those souls out there. You have to be that salt and light to others, the only way you can do that is through seeking the good of others, and should you do that, you will be able to help souls to be saved.

"Even as I try to please everybody in every way. For I am not seeking my own good but the good of many, so that they may be saved." {1Corinthains 10:33 }

"Accept one another, then, just as Christ accepted you, in order to bring praise to God. For I tell you that Christ has become a servant of the Jews on behalf of God's truth, to confirm the promises made to the patriarchs so that the Gentiles may glorify God for his mercy." {*Romans 15:7-9*}

Saved to Serve

God is a God of works. Our Lord said:

"My father is always at his work to this very day, ànd I, too am working"
{John 5:17}

"My Father works even now" He is the God who works all things after the counsel of His will. But God does not do everything directly by himself.

He works through his servants. If we look at how God used to reveal His work, He was always using His servants the prophets.

"Surely the sovereign Lord does nothing without revealing his plan to his servant's the prophets." *{Amos 3:7}*

Someone who is a serving servant in the ministry of the Lord is someone who is very much Helpful, who do things as it is expected out of him. He is someone who is in demand and in need by the others who are around him. He doesn't disappoint he does things as it is expected out of him.

"Only Luke is with me. Get Mark and bring him with you, because he is helpful to me in my ministry. I sent Tychich to Ephesus." {2 Timothy 4:11-12}

"And I sent them to Iddo, the leader in Casiphia, I told them what to say to Iddo and his kinsmen, the temple servants in Casiphia, so that they might bring attendant's to us for the house of our God. Because the gracious hand of our God was on us, they brought Sherebiah, a capable man..." {Ezra 8:17-18}

There are servants in the temple of the Lord, those who serve the others according to their needs. In the fullness of time God sent his Son into the world to do his work. He is known as Christ, that is, the **Anointed one**.

As the term **Son** means him as a person, and the name **Christ** means the office He as Jesus He was holding.

Though he was the son of God, He was sent to be the Christ of God, that means to come and hold a specific office on earth. He had a divine commission to accomplish. So Jesus did not just come on earth on his own, but came for a specific mission, he had a ministry that he was chosen and sent for to do. In that, He took the position of a servant.

While He was on earth. He was aware that his time on earth was limited, so as he was busy with the work that was entrusted to Him by the Father in heaven,

He prepared some people to continue His work after His departure. As God was using the prophets to reveal himself and his plans, for us.

"Come and follow me, Jesus said; and I will make you the fishers of man."

{Matthew 4:19}

These men he chose; later on, they became known as the Apostles. They were the chosen ones. And Jesus used them to carry on spreading the gospel and to do all that He has done in front of them.

"As you sent me into the world, I have sent them into the world." {John17:18}

We have been given kindness undeserving favour by God to be saved, and God accepted us through his, grace according to the measure of the gift of Christ. So that we can serve him and his people through our gifts.

"But to each one of us grace has been given as Christ apportioned it." {Ephesians 4:7}

He has given gifts to men. He has given some to be the Apostles, some Prophets, some Evangelist, Shepherds and Teachers for the perfecting of the saints, with a view to the work of the ministry for the building up of the body of Christ.

Those gifts Jesus gave them, were not just the gifts for them to do as they wish but they were given it, so that they can use it in the house of the Lord Jesus Christ and serving the saints.

"It was he who gave some to be Apostles, some to be Prophets, some to be Evangelist and some to be Pastors and Teachers. To prepare Gods people for works of service, so that the body of Christ may be built up." {Ephesians 4:11-12}

There are many ministries connected with the service of God. He chooses a number of men for special ministries. The ministry of the word of God for the building up of the body of Christ. Since that ministry is different from others. It is neither a one-man ministry or an all-man ministry. But a ministry based upon the gift of the Holy Spirit and an experimental knowledge of the Lord.

Apostles, Prophets, Evangelists, Pastors and Teachers are our Lords gifts to His Church to serve in the ministry according to offices they are holding.

An office is that which one is received as the result of a commission.

God desires a service of His children. But He makes conscripts. He wants people who will do the job wholeheartedly. The work is His; He is the only legitimate originator.

Human intention, however good, cannot take the place of divine initiation. Earnest desires for the salvation of sinners or the edification of saints will never qualify a man for Gods work.

One qualification, and only one is necessary: God must send him.

You remember how Barnabas and Paul were chosen; it was the Holy Spirit that called them to the ministry. They were not called because of the man's desires or interests, but it's the Spirit of the Lord from the Lord God Himself that wanted them to go and do the work.

"While they were worshiping the Lord and fasting, the Holy Spirit said " set apart for me Barnabas and Saul for the work to which I have called them". {Acts 13:2}.

Only the Divine call can qualify a person to take a lead in the office ministry.

The saddest part in Christian work today is that many workers that have gone out there, they have not been sent. Personal desires, friendly persuasions, the advice of one's elders and the urge of opportunities; all these factors on the natural plane and they can never take the place of the Spiritual call. Calling must be something that comes from the Spirit of God.

"And how can they preach unless they are sent?" {Romans 10:15}

When Barnabas and Paul were sent off by the brothers in the church, it was the Spirit of God that called them first, then the brothers confirmed their call.

Brothers at church they may say you have a call, and circumstances may seem to indicate that, but the question is, have you yourself heard the call?

If you have to go on, then you are the one who should first hear the voice of the Spirit. We don't undermine the opinion of the brothers, but their opinion must not substitute a personal call from God.

If God desires the service of any child of His, He himself will call him to it and He Himself will send him to go and do the work. So the first requirement in divine work is a divine call.

Everything starts with this. A divine call gives God His rightful place, for it recognises Him as the originator of the work. Where there is no call from God, the work undertaken is not divine original from God and it contains no Spiritual value.

Divine work must be divinely initiated. A worker may be called directly by the Spirit. Or indirectly through the reading of the Word, through preaching or through circumstances.

That is why Jesus even said that those who want to follow Him they must take up their cross, because He was aware that along His way, as He keeps on with His ministry, there would be others except the one's He called who will also want to follow him. He said they would have to take up their cross, because taking a cross it will demand a lot from them in serving Him and his people.

"If anyone would come after me, he must deny himself and take up his cross daily and follow me." {Luke 9:23}

But whatever means God may use to make His will known to man, God will use it. God my Lord has no specific formula in doing His own will. It doesn't matter how educated or if you are a scholar, because we people, we have that tendency of thinking and wanting to see the things of the Lord my God happening according to our point of views. I'm so sorry about those who use their education thinking that they know the things of my Lord Jesus Christ.

"For the wisdom of this world is foolishness with God. For it is written, He catches the wise in their own craftiness." {1 Corinthians 3: 19}

It is no wonder we experience what we are experiencing in our denominations, because we have put God behind us, and focused on our education. Busy claiming that we have studied this.

If I may ask; is it your studies that make you not to tell the people of God about the Holiness of your congregants?

But all that I know is, God is not a respecter of man. And no one can tell Him how to do things, there is just no way the creation can tell its creator on how to do things. Our duty is to be submissive and obedient with acceptance.

"Who was I to think that I can oppose God?" {Acts 11:17}

We see the brothers confronting Peter to explain why those people at Cornelius house were baptised with the Holy Spirit, because to them all they knew was that a person must be baptised with water first then with the Holy Spirit; for getting what the Lord said:

"For John baptised with water, but in a few days you will be baptised with the Holy Spirit." {Acts 1:5}

But the most important thing is, His voice must be the one heard through every other voice. He must be the one who speaks no matter through what instrument the call may come. We must never be independent from other members of the body. But we must never forget that we receive all our direct orders from God.

Therefore: It is the responsibility of every man who claims to be saved to serve the Lord accordingly and to Gods own interest. It is a brother's duty and privilege to serve the Lord. God intended that every Christian should be a "Christian Worker".

So, what does that really mean?

That clearly shows us that if you are a Child of God you are expected to do something in the house of the Lord and to people in your surrounding area. If you care to notice around you, in your street, you will see children playing all sorts of games; some are nasty games. As an adult and mostly as a Christian, what do you do when you see those kids?

Don't you go to them and collect them together and do something constructive that will build them up for a better tomorrow and mostly help them to grow in knowing that Jesus Christ is the Lord and no other Lord like Christ Jesus.

"The King will reply, I tell you the truth, whatever you did for one of the least of these brothers of mine, you did it for me." {*Matthew 25:40*}

When you are serving, you must serve with humility and humbleness being an example to others.

Let us look at Jesus the Lord {**John 13:1**}. If you notice the last part of the verse it says: *"He now showed them the full extent of his love."*

Can you see?

Jesus did not just do what he did for the sake of doing it, he did it to the full extent of his love, he gave it all not just. Again, as we said you must set an example to others, so that they can see what is also expected from them to do.

"I have set you an example that you should do as I have done for you" *{John 13:15}*.

There must be that growing desire even if there are things that may seem to deem along the way, but just because of that zeal and the love for God you have; press on moving forward with positiveness.

"Then Caleb silenced the people before Moses and said, we should go up take possession of the land, for we can certainly do it." *{Numbers 13:30}*

"Never be lacking in zeal, but keep your spiritual fervour, serving the Lord"
{Romans 12:11}.

You press on serving the Lord because you know that working for the Lord is not in vain you don't let challenges to drag you down, you press on doing things for the Lord.

"Because you know that your labour in the Lord is not in vain." {1 Corinthians 15:58}

And when you are serving, you have a vision and a purpose of wanting to achieve something at the end, and that vision is the one that will make you to keep on serving and doing what is expected.

"The man who plants and the man who waters have one purpose, and each will be rewarded according to his own labour ". {1 Corinthians 3:8}

You see that eagerness and willingness they had within them, of wanting to go and do the job of searching for Elijah; you don't relax, even though you see things are not going well in the house of the Lord and to His people.

" But they persisted until he was too ashamed to refuse." {2 Kings 2:17}

That is the heart that each and every single individual should carry in his/ her spiritual life, as long as they claim that they are God's children.

Serving in the Lord should be inspired by the love for God and his people, serving faithfully and wholeheartedly, knowing that whatever he/she is doing. He /she is Serving for Gods glory. They must watch themselves and their footstep that where ever they go, Jesus Christ the Lord is seen in them.

"How beautiful on the mountains are the feet of those who bring good news, who proclaim peace, who bring good tidings, who proclaim salvation, who say to Zion, "Your God reigns!" {Isaiah 52:7}

Therefore, what is expected out of someone who serve in the Lord is Humbleness, humanity, word of command and mostly above all, Love.

"Offer hospitality to one another without grumbling. Each one should use whatever gift he has received to serve others, faithfully administering God's grace in its various forms. If anyone speaks, he should do it as one speaking the very same words of God. If anyone serves; he should do it with the strength God provides, so that in all things God may be praised through Jesus Christ. To him be the glory and the power forever and ever. Amen." {1 Peter 4: 9-11}

Therefore, serving in the Lord; there are certain requirements that someone needs to acquire in order to be a good servant and to serve in the house of the Lord, specifically if that person claims he is a born-again child of God and is saved. He must be watchful of himself and how he walks.

"If a man cleansed himself from the latter, he will be an instrument for noble purposes, made holy, useful to the master and prepared to do any good work." {2Timothy 2:21}

Yes; along the way to what you are or what you want to do, there would be people who will want to stand and be the stumbling blocks along your way.

But due to the fact that you yourself knows that you are not all alone in this, you have God with you, and with the strong conviction in you, you will stand boldly for the work of the Lord.

"But Peter and John replied, "Judge for yourselves whether it is right in God sight to obey you rather than God. For we cannot help speaking about what we have seen and heard." {Acts 4: 19-20}

As we have said before, that you don't relax in the house of the Lord, it costs a lot to follow Jesus. In the house of the Lord people with fine eyes and ears are needed to safe guard and protect what belongs to the Lord, because amongst us there are those who have not just came to the house of the Lord to praise and worshiped God, but there are the devil worshipers. They are there to destroy God's people, so those people who have spiritual eyes and ears, they protect and see and hear things and prevent anything to happen in the house of the Lord Jesus Christ.

"During the time Mordecai was sitting at the king's gate, Bigthana and Teresh, two of the king's officers who guarded the doorway, became angry and conspired to assassinate King Xerxes. But Mordecai found out about the plot and told Queen Esther, who in turn reported it to the King, giving credit to Mordecai." {Esther 2:21-23).

"'My food,' said Jesus, 'is to do the will of him who sent me and to finish his work'." {John 4:34}

Take a Lead

The word "Leader" means someone who takes the lead. Taking the '**Lead**' means leading and giving guidance to the ones he leads. When taking the lead, there are rivers (challenges) you should cross so that you as a leader, you would know what to expect for the people you will lead.

So you as a leader, you must have a personal experience in things; those experiences will build your character. In your challenges that you have experienced there will always be ways out or solutions in whatever you are encountering.

Let's take an example of Moses. Moses led God's people and God was with him all the way. {NB: Joshua 1:1-7 - NOTE WELL verse 7}

We have been given a redeemer to redeem us and save the world from its iniquities, Lord Jesus Christ. He came to be a living example of what the Lord God wants out of us, so that we may follow in His footsteps, because Jesus is a leader. He had to lead us by an example so that we may do as He has shown us.

"I have set you an example that you should do as I have done for you" {John 13:15}

Talking about taking a lead in the house of the Lord, that can surely mean that we have also to look at a leader. A gift of leadership is comparatively rare to exercise and very often it takes a great deal of courage and the successful achievement of one's ambition or goal is generally the aim and desire of everyone.

"Because of the hand of the Lord my God was on me, I took courage and gathered leading men from Israel to go up with me." {Ezra 7:28}

If you feel ready to accept the responsibility of leadership, it is of vital importance that you place yourself in God's hands. The greatest leader of all times, and the one upon whom the heaviest burden of responsibility rested, was Jesus Christ. And He succeeded because His faith in God was firm and unshakable.

If you follow His example, you will find that God will give you courage and the ability to fulfil the role of a leader. He will guide you and give you a sense of peace that will enable you to overcome all fears and doubts as you follow him.

That is what a leader is, to guide, give peace, motivate and to uplift its people.

Let us just take a look to **NEHEMIAH**.

Who was he? Nehemiah was a servant of a Persian King Artaxerxes 1. He was so moved by the situation in Palestine in 444 BC, he asked for permission from his king to return to the land of his forefathers to rebuild the walls.

Seemingly, out of nowhere one of the most effective leaders in the bible would appear in stage of history. In two months' time, he managed to accomplish what was neglected by others for almost a century.

The walls were rebuilt and Israel took a giant step forward towards becoming an independent nation once again. Nehemiah is not just a book of leaders. His great leadership qualities encourage and have a great influence to every Christian in these days.

"When the people heard this, they were cut to the heart and said to Peter and the other apostles, 'Brothers; what shall we do?'" {Acts 2:37}

Is there anything that cuts through to your heart? Is there any consciousness in you? Are you repenting? Nehemiah, he was honest about his sin and to himself. Why he was like that?

Because to him, Nehemiah knew that in order for him to lead people to repentance, he himself he must be an example.

Can you still remember, what Jesus also did to the disciples? He showed them an example. So as Nehemiah did, there are people who have a tendency to tell people to confess and what they must do, but on the other side they don't do what they preach to others.

"I confess, the sins we Israelites, including myself and my father's house, have committed against you. We have not obeyed the commands, decrees and laws you gave your servant Moses." {Nehemiah 1:6-7}

He saw his sin, and saw it as wicked. He had courage to look at himself and repent. Some hide sins instead of seeking help. Some talk to themselves when they are in a bad situation or having some misunderstanding with someone, instead of going to the people who have done them wrong and talk about the problem.

Some won't even take a challenge seriously, pride, marriage and lack of intensity. Nehemiah, showed a great faith and took an initiative. He believed that no matter how scattered they were and bad the situation it was.

God is there and gives the victory. One way to never lose faith, is to keep your eyes on the one and only, the awesome God. What he did, instead, he wanted to give up his job and go out to wilderness to go and correct the situation, with a great belief.

Nehemiah was a nobody. He had no visions like John and he worked no miracles like the apostles. He was just a normal man, and yet his courage and determination were inspiring. If we take a greater look at Nehemiah, he never forgets to pray.

Prayer open doors. He surveys the situation of the land. When you lead you must gather some more information and spend some time focusing on the task ahead of you.

When you are to lead, you must have a way of communicating and approaching people, and you will see their response of willingness and you have to plan things well. Be prepared to face opposition, because when Gods people get up and get busy, oppositions starts quickly. So do not let opposition steal your zeal. {Nehemiah 2: 4-19}

In chapter 3, it is so amazing how Nehemiah was effective at every level, because he was organised. In order to be organised, you must have the value of the time. Get organized with people, let them feel important, because they are. You have to know when they are sick, birthdays and their anniversaries.

Noticing and caring is crucial to anyone who is intending to lead.

Let them feel appreciated by you, by praising and encouraging their strengths and victories. Be a good listener.

"We who are strong ought to bear with the failings of the weak and not to please ourselves. Each of us should please his neighbour for his good, to build him up." {Romans 15: 1-2}.

When you are going to lead, you must be prepared that you will turn the weaknesses into strength, obstacles into stepping stones and disaster into triumph. And face the music even when the tune is not good.

Though Nehemiah was an ordinary person, he had in him an extraordinary determination.

In Chapter 4, it seems that everything was not going right, things were going wrong, there were some obstacles along their way. Their enemies were getting angry, started to stand in front of their plan, they were mocked publicly by their enemies when they saw the work that was done by Nehemiah and his man.

They started becoming angry and started planning disruptions that resulted in Nehemiah's labourers starting to give up the work because they were faced with some death threats, obstacles, cowards and all sorts of things.

But not to Nehemiah; all those things didn't make him scared and feel under pressured, but rather he put his trust unto the Lord God almighty and continued with the work.

"But you, keep your head in all situations, endure hardship, do the work of an evangelistic, discharge all the duties of your ministry." {2 Timothy 4: 5}

Nehemiah prayed and prayed, kept on surveying the job and continuing with his plan, motivating his troops with rousing speeches to trust in the Lord. And they got back to work. He didn't retreat or give up, he pressed on moving forward, because he knew deep down that he have a duty to accomplish. He stands firm.

Is there any plan that you follow when you are faced with challenges? Or do you give up, give in, and give out?

"He called you to this through our gospel, that you might share in the glory of our Lord Jesus Christ. So then, brothers, stand firm and hold to the teachings we passed to you, whether by word of mouth or by letter". {2 Thessalonians 2 :14-15}

Our challenge to win the world came to us in order to lead Gods people in knowing Him, and showing them how they ought to conduct themselves in the Lord.

In order that to happen we have to look deep down on us if we are what is needed to lead Gods people, are we humbled, considerate and filled with love for others.

"As a prisoner for the Lord, then, I urge you to live a life worthy of the calling you have received. Be completely humble and gentle; be patient, bearing with one another in love." *{Ephesians 4:1-2}*

In order to be that person, you must have the attitude of 'Lord make me an instrument of your peace. Where there is hatred, let me sow love. Where there is injury, pardon. Where there is doubt, faith. Where there is despair, hope. Where there is darkness, light. And where there is sadness, joy.'

A caring person is an elevated person. It is a great act of kindness to express your caring for people who might not realise that you care about them.

If you will lead God's people, you will need to possess good great qualities and be a man of high character. It doesn't matter how good a man preaches, or how prominent he is in the community. If his personal life or his family life is out of order, he is not qualified to lead God's people.

"Here is a trustworthy saying: If anyone set his heart on being an overseer, he desires a noble task. Now the overseer must be above reproach, the husband of but one wife, temperate, self -controlled, respectable, Hospitable, able to teach, not given to drunkenness, not violent but gentle, not quarrelsome, not a lover of money. He must manage his own family well and see that his children obey him with proper respect. (If anyone does not know how to manage his own family, how can He take care of God's Church?) He must not be a recent convert, or he may become conceited and fall under the same judgement as the devil." {1 Timothy 3: 1-5&6}

Why Paul is talking like this? If you remember well in **John 13: 15.**

The Lord Jesus Christ set an example to His disciples; He didn't just teach them something that He is not doing himself. So to lead God's people you should be an example, because the people that you will lead will observe your movements and take whatever you do and imitate you. And they won't be blamed by imitating you and your ways, because the word of God itself allows them to do so, to imitate you, so when you do not do right, that would mean, you have misled them.

"Remember your leaders, who spoke the word of God to you. Consider the outcome of their way of life and imitate their faith." {Hebrews 13: 7}

Taking a lead, it must be a divine call, with developed character and deep convictions. When you have these within you, you will stand firm in any challenge you face and overcome any temptation you come across with. Because you are rooted, when rooted with conviction, you will always be aware and see things when they come you will have a spiritual eye that will make you awake and alert at all times. And you will be able to look even after those you lead.

"Keep watch over yourselves and all the flock of which the Holy Spirit has made you overseers, be shepherds of the church of God, which He bought with his own blood." {Acts 20:28}

Expect

When God created man on earth, He didn't create a man without any good reason or any plan, and His plan was not to harm a man,or to make a man suffer ;since a man is the reflection of his image and He wanted a man to have no other hope but only to Him as God and God is assuring man that he will listen, God listen to prayers.

"'For I know the plans I have for you,' declares the Lord, 'plans to prosper you and not to harm you, plans to give you hope and a future. Then you will call upon me and come and pray to me I will listen to you. You will seek me and find me when you seek me with all your heart. I will be found by you', declares the Lord, 'and will bring you back from captivity.'"
{Jeremiah 29:11-14}

So where else can we run and turn too, except him? God is our hope and we have already mentioned what is hope is; hope is nothing else except that it is the signal of faith that is made certain of the things that we don't see.

It is also a feeling of expecting things to go well {optimism}, a thought that says things will improve, things will go in a positive way for me. It won't always be miserable, dark; there is always a way to rise above the present terrible circumstances.

Hope is an internal awareness that you do not have to suffer forever, and that somehow, somewhere there is a remedy in feeling hopeless. {Despair}.

That you will come upon if you can only maintain this expectancy in your heart.

For it is in the presence of a hopeful vision that hopelessness and suffering no longer hold our attention. That's where faith comes in.

"Now faith is being sure of what we hope for and certain of what we do not see" {Hebrews 11:1}

We all have dreams and wishes, and mostly expectations of getting the things we wish and need in our lives; we pray day and night to the Almighty God to help us to achieve what we want in our lives.

Sometimes as we pray, we are sometimes filled with doubts that God is not hearing our prayers and sometimes we even come to a point that God is not answering our prayers. We start being filled with doubts that maybe there is somewhere, where we are not doing good to please Him, or we don't receive because we are not worthy to Him to receive anything. We start to be filled with all those doubts; no, my friend, it is not like that.

"For God does not show favouritism." {Romans 2:11}

God hears and answers every prayer of those who trust and believe in Him.

"Trust in the Lord with all your heart and lean not on your own understanding." {Proverbs 3:5}

Those who trust in Him will never be put in shame, If we lean not on our understanding, we will not carry on struggling and suffer on our own, we will take every challenge we face to Him who our hope is, the only thing is to strive and put our struggles to him.

"And for this we labour and strive, that we have put our hope in the living God, who is the Saviour of all men, and especially of those who believe." {1 Timothy 4:10}

So when we have someone we know is there for us, that means we can have hope in Him; we don't panic, we relax.

"But if we hope for what we do not yet have, we wait for it patiently." {Romans 8:25}

Why? Because God has better things for us, more than we can imagine. And those who trust in Him will never be put in shame. As the scripture says:

"Anyone who trust in him will never be put to shame". {Romans 10: 11}

"God had planned something better for us so that only together with us would they be made perfect." {Hebrews 11: 40}

"Gods promise is not slack. The Lord is not slow in keeping his promise, as some understand slowness. He is patient with you, not wanting anyone to perish, but everyone to come to repentance." {2 Peter 3: 9}

All we need to have with us is to have strong faith deep in our hearts. Faith is the victory of knowing that God is with us and we have the power of overcoming our struggles; that is the greatest positive thing that we have, that makes us not to live in doubts about ourselves but to push and press on, for we know that we will overcome.

"For everyone born of God overcomes the world, this is the victory that has overcome the world, even our faith. Who is it that overcomes the world? Only, he who believes that Jesus is the Son of God." {1 John 5: 4-5 }

When you know that you have a power to overcome the world, that gives us the knowledge that there is a solution in everything we do, whereby we have God our saviour, who hears and listen to our prayer's day and night.

That makes us only not to have doubts in the Lord, but be filled with High Expectations that whatever we pray for in Him, He will reward us, so there is no need that we can't expect from our creator.

"He replied, 'Because you have so little faith, I tell you the truth, if you have faith as small as a mustard seed, you can say to this mountain, 'Move from here to there, and it will move'." {Matthew 17: 20}

"This is the confidence we have in approaching God: that if we ask anything according to his will, he hears us. And if we know that he hears us---whatever we ask---we know that we have what we asked of him". {1 John 5:14-15}

Every beginning, as today, is God's opportunity to confirm His word in your life, with daily loads of benefits, those benefits come through your prayers. Those benefits come beyond your imaginations. You shall not go empty! But not without a demand from you to God in every area you desire.

To fully reap the benefits of prayer, we must fully believe in the one in whom we are praying to. Our God is not only a prayer hearing God, but mostly; He is also a prayer answering God.

When you understand the importance and higher purposes of prayer, you will always be willing and excited to pray, you pray up to the point of praying in tongues. One of the beautiful things the Holy Spirit has done in our lives as God's children is to give us the ability to speak even in tongues.

Take your personal and corporate time of prayer very seriously. Create the opportunities in the course of your day fellowshipping with the Lord through prayer, and your life will flourish from glory to glory.

Here we can look at some of the few benefits of prayer that we can expect from God.

BENEFITS OF PRAYER:

1) <u>Peace of mind</u>:

The solution to the problem of the day is the awakening of the consciousness of humanity to the divinity within.

"Do not be anxious over anything, but in everything by prayer and petition, with all thanksgiving, present your request to God. And the peace of God, which transcends all understanding, will guard your hearts and your minds in Christ Jesus" {Philippians 4: 6-7}

2) <u>Comfort from God</u>:

As children of the Almighty God, we are blessed with the promise of perfect peace. The peace that comes from God surpasses our understanding and allows us to experience hope, blessing, strength and joy.

We serve a gracious God of peace, who promises to take care of us, comfort us provide for us and restore our hope and joy.

Since God is the Father who comforts us in ALL of our tribulations, we should not believe Him in other things and not to others. This means that there should be no situations or circumstances that you believe you can handle things on your own and limit our God.

When we receive comfort from God, we are then able to pass it to others by the word of our testimony. That is the comfort of the confidence that we have through our meaning full prayers.

"Praise be to God and Father of our Lord Jesus Christ, the Father of compassion and the God of all comfort, who comfort us in all our troubles, so that we can comfort those in any trouble with the comfort we ourselves have received from God". {2 Corinthians 1 :3-4}

"Therefore, do not worry about tomorrow, for tomorrow will worry about itself. Each day has enough troubles of its own". {Matthew 6: 34}

3) <u>Confidence</u>:

It builds self -assurance and trust and build boldness character in you that what you want will happen.

"Do not be like them, for your Father knows what you need before you ask him." {Matthew 6:8}

"If you believe, you will receive whatever you ask for in prayer." {Matthew 21: 22}

"You may ask me for anything in my name, I will do it." {John 14: 14}

What is it that is in your mind, that is bothering and making you wondering around and not moving forward in getting and achieving what you are expecting in your life?

Is your mind filled with doubts, do you see things as if they are impossible to happen? If you have a strong positive faith in God, you won't even bother yourself with much things, instead you will go forward and persuade whatever you want in your life, irrespective of what the obstacles are in front of you.

"Because she thought, "If I just touch his clothes, I will be healed. Immediately her bleeding stopped and she felt in her body that she was freed from her suffering" {Mark 5: 28-29}

A man of God, a man who really knows who the Lord is, and knows that in him the Lord everything is possible, he expects with faith that God will just say the word and things will happen.

Remember, God when he created the world, he just said the word and everything was there; so when you are expecting from the Lord you must have spiritual ears and listen to what the Lord will say. And when you have those spiritual ears, you won't hesitate to go and do according to what the Lord has told you.

"That is why I did not even consider myself worthy to come to you. But say the word, and my servant will be healed." {*Luke 7:7*}

How I so wish that we can have Christians who can be ready and be prepared to hear what the word of God says, and walk according to it in these last days. People who won't walk with their sight, but by faith in the Lords word.

When you walk with faith in the Lord, you wait in him as you are expecting. Those who expect they wait into the Lord; they don't push up things to happen as they want or as they wish in their own time. Instead, they delight everything in the Lord. All you need is to wait unto the Lord.

The reason why we don't get what we want and expect in our lives is that we are not patient; we don't wait patiently unto the Lord, though everything is in his hands.

"Delight yourself in the Lord and he will give you the desires of your heart."
{Psalms 37:4}

When expecting from the lord, you must develop within you a positive undivided attention in the Lord, that what you are asking for, you will probably get it undoubtedly without any hesitations through the Lord Jesus Christ.

"So the man gave them his attention, expecting to get something from them."
{Acts 3:5}

In getting and expecting Gods blessings it needs someone to have a positive mind set, and put to death the old mind, because the old one is full of negative thoughts that are dwelling in your past weaknesses.

Your biggest battle can produce your greater breakthrough. Don't be scared of the stress you are passing through it in pursuing your dreams. Always know that your tomorrow will never be like your yesterday. There is a huge greatness in you, and if you refuse to birth it out, you will never get 'there' from 'here'.

Be empowered and encouraged today by the knowledge that you have your God with you to expect from, you have to the high expectations in your life. Stop living in your comfort zone and start doing what will bring out the best of your version.

You are a great vessel, with an unexplainable expected vision. I want you to know that to be the great version that you are. You must achieve your vision, because that is what you are expecting in your life all because you know what your God will do for you.

Why? A ten thousand kilometres race, it at all begins with one step forward. Stop looking back at your past failures and begin looking forward to tomorrow's success, for that is what you are destined for by God.

Your yesterday will never come back no matter how you try. When you keep dwelling to your past, you will keep on dwelling on your failures. You are not a failure, until you start thinking about failures. Even to what you are experiencing now, don't ask why things are like this, why things are not like yesterday.

"Do not say, 'Why were the old days better than these?' For it is not wise to ask such questions." {Ecclesiastes 7: 10}

Don't be discouraged about your life. Don't be guilty of your yesterday's mistakes. You can still be a complete man or woman. You know what I like most about the past, it gives a great experience in order that you can be a living example to others, you can manage to tell and teach others about what you know best with an experience you have. Therefore; my friend, you can still do right again from now onwards.

"Do not be quickly provoked in your spirit, for anger resides in the lap of fools."
{Ecclesiastes 7: 9}

It is not all about who you were in the past, but it is all about the positive expectations that you are presently having today for your life tomorrow. However, when you take decisions into fruition, that is fruitful decisions.

A decision taken that is not pushed with actions always ends up fading away. Take action today and expect from God. You will never regret when you will see yourself landing in tomorrow.

What is your plan today? Stand up and start doing what you have to do. Strengthen and revive your prayer life and your determination. Don't think about any Satan. Satan have no power over you, because you know whom you are trusting and expecting greater things from, for you don't live in the past, you are the child of God.

It is no wonder why the scriptures say that anyone who is born again is a new creation; the old one has gone, that means even your thinking change.

"To be made new in the attitude of your minds." {*Ephesians* 4:23}

Therefore, brothers and sisters:

"Do not conform any longer to the pattern of this world, but be transformed by the renewing of your mind. Then you will be able to test and approve what God's will is---his good and pleasing and perfect will." {*Romans 12:2*}

There is nothing; I mean nothing you can expect to get from the Lord ;if you don't have faith in him, you don't know what his will is for you and should you come to know his will about you, what you are asking for. You will get it, all you need is to grow deep down in your faith.

"Be patient, then brothers, until the Lord 's coming. See how the farmer waits for the land to yield its valuable crop and how patient he is for the autumn and spring rains. You too, be patient and stand firm, because the Lord's coming is near.

Don't grumble against each other, brothers, or you will be judged. The Judge is standing at the door! Brothers, as an example of patience in the face of suffering, take the prophets who spoke in the name of the Lord. As you know, we consider blessed those who have persevered. You have heard of Jobs perseverance and have seen what the Lord finally brought about. The Lord is full of compassion and mercy. Above all, my brothers, do not swear----not by heaven or by earth or by anything else. Let your "Yes" be "Yes" and your "No", "No", or you will be condemned." {James 5: 7-12}

AMEN..........

Praise be to God the Lord Jesus Christ!!!!!!

The End

"Greatness of God cannot be measured by time, circumstances or by anyone. But by the wonders of His work, that displays that firmament, which our lives can depend on Him".

Luthando Ningiza

9 781990 940118